WHITE TURK
vs
BLACK TURK

Roots of Political Schism in Turkey

"An extraordinary magnum opus generating awareness on the poisonous effects of political hatred corrupting Turkish democratic climate.

An essential reference for academics, think tanks, politicians, students of political science and diplomats interested in Türkiye and for every person hating hatred."

Prof. Dr. Fahri Erenel
Brig. General (Ret)

WHITE TURK
vs
BLACK TURK

Roots of Political Schism in Turkey

Aydın Nurhan

WHITE TURK
vs
BLACK TURK

Roots of Political Schism in Turkey

AYDIN NURHAN
Ambassador (R)

Copyright © 2023 by Aydın Nurhan.

This publication is in copyright. No reproduction of any part may take place without the written permission of its author.

© 2023, AYDIN NURHAN
Work: WHITE TURK vs BLACK TURK
Roots of Political Schism in Turkey
Author: Aydın Nurhan
Cover Design: Nevin Ece Nurhan
ISBN: 978-1-917095-75-4
1st Edition: August 2023
E-mail: aydin.nurhan@yahoo.com

WHITE TURK versus BLACK TURK
Roots of Political Schism in Turkey
AYDIN NURHAN
Ambassador (R)
ISTANBUL – 2023

In memory of my late father, Ekrem Nurhan

Sultan and the Tiger

Thirty-six Ottoman Sultans:

Twelve toppled,
Six murdered.

In the Republic:

One President and
Ten Prime Ministers were overthrown by military coups,
One President survived an assassination attempt,
One President died in mystery,
One Prime Minister and three Ministers were hanged…

Those who reign on the back of the tiger…
Can not avoid being its prey one day.

- Uğur Mumcu

The only condition for living with the tiger is to be its master.
You are either the master or the prey.

- Zülfü Livaneli
"On the Back of the Tiger"

Table of Contents

THANKS i
FOREWORD iii
CONCEPTS viii
   Bourgeois ix
   Lumpen x
   Devshirme x
   Türkmen xi
   Ataturk xii
   15 July 2016 Democracy Day xvi
INTRODUCTION 2
   Transformation 2
PART ONE 8
   Psychology 8
   Conformism 17
   Extraordinariness 30
   Political Psychology 31
   Political Preference 35
   Modernists 40
   Conservatives 59
PART TWO 63
   Ottoman Empire 63
   Devshirme Bureaucracy 73
   Reâyâ (Periphery) 79

Janissary Revolts 83

Guild Revolts 86

Celali Revolts 89

Suhte Revolts 95

Tanzimat 95

PART THREE 98

Early Republic 98

Class Consciousness - Beginnings of Conflict 100

Bloodless Revolution of the Turk 108

Founding Father of Turkish Democracy 109

Reactionary Counter-Revolution 110

Turkmen to the Mission 112

Bourgeoisie 116

Modern Politics 121

The USA - Catalyst of the Turkish Democratic Revolution 128

Presidential System 130

Changing Roles 134

The Unclaimed State 137

Media 143

Identity in the Republic 147

Our Identity Elements 150

National Dream 153

Our Kurds 154

Our Turkish Language 157

Religion 161

The Need for Dogma 172

Law 174
　　Literature and Music 177
　　Education 181
　　Digested Information 186
　　Teacher Quality 189
　　The Speed of Materialism 190
　　Enderun/University 192
　　Foreign Affairs 193
　　Business 197
　　Corporatism 199
　　And Finally Atatürk 199
ADVICE TO YOUTH 208
CONCLUSION 211
RESOURCES 216
ABOUT THE AUTHOR 226

THANKS

Writing my book, I requested the advice and criticisms of some of our distinguished professors, whose academic discipline and morals I respect. They spent their precious time to read my manuscripts and gave their insights. I cannot give enough thanks to Ahmet Taşağıl, Ahmet Sedat Aybar, Ekrem Erdem, Erol Göka, Fahri Erenel and Mehmet Seyfettin Erol in alphabetical order. I should note that the onus is on me for the shortcomings in my book, not on them. I should also express that we are in different positions with my dear professors in many intellectual fields. What is beautiful and moral is that, brains with very different judgments may need each other's knowledge and benefit from each other.

Many authors rightly mention family members in the dedication and acknowledgement sections of their books. Family is indeed sacred. It is the most precious asset for human beings. Going with the tradition, my gratitude to my mother Meliha Nurhan and my late father, Ekrem Nurhan, who made me who I am. Also, to my wife Betül, my life partner of fifty-five years, my dear brother Said, my daughter Nevin Ece Nurhan who designed the cover graphics of my book, as well to my son Ekrem Nurhan who advised me on academic matters. As a member of this beautiful family, I live in paradise in this world.

And finally, thanks to my dear and lovely assistant İsmail Ararut, and my friend and Turkish editor İhsan Toy, who contributed to the preparation of the Turkish original of this book for publication and who took much trouble with my ceaseless renewals.

Special thanks, of course, to my English editor Audrey Hope and my project manager Isaac Levine as well as to all the staff at Amazon Publishing Pros, who provided technical support for the publication of my book.

FOREWORD

The seed of this paper is my late father's advice: "Always be with the oppressed."

In my seventy-four years, I have realised that people who humiliate, look down upon, and insult others, have some deficiency. They are in an insatiable thirst for respect. They crave dignity. They have rigid defence shields against being ridiculed and avoided. And from what I've read in books, they have a perpetual longing for "love and warm embrace", which was denied to many of them in infancy.

So long as the search for reverence remains personal, it does not pose a social problem. Yet the demand for prestige, hunger for acceptance in society, and inferiority complex go beyond individual crave and become transmitted into a social setting; it poisons politics and leads to detrimental dimensions for national unity.

Search for social prestige shows itself in two opposing lifestyles: Conservative/traditional lifestyle versus Western/modern lifestyle. From the Ottoman Tanzimat (Westernization) of the 19th Century to the present, we see that the dominant lifestyle of power holders in Türkiye is the Western lifestyle. This elite, strategically supported by Western powers, claim the right to look down upon the underdog and feel assigned a duty by the West for a forced "mission civilisatrice" upon their people. An act of internal orientalism.

Famous Turkish leftist poet and thinker late Attila İlhan called such elite as "cultural compradors" of the West.1[1]

Of the historically oppressed underdog of the periphery, some expected that if they chose the imposed Westernization, they might also join the class of the ruling elites of the country. And some did. But they had to be slaves to a certain convention. Let alone questioning or challenging it, even a minor distrust or hesitation on Western world view was heresy ending in ostracism from the elite powerhouse. And excommunication and exclusion were not a bearable pain. To be branded as a peasant, religious zealot, regressive, hick, or enemy of progress, was a terrible punishment, especially in the lumpen arts and sports community. Hence such aspirants were scared and terrorised to toe the line.

This essay intends to search for the roots of the clashing lifestyles in Türkiye that lead to polarisation in the Turkish political arena with factors coming from the depths of history. It also focuses primarily on the psychological and socio-psychological aspects of the conflict.

The endeavour actually started as a rich-referenced semi-academic study in English for Westerners who had a prejudiced view of Türkiye. The aim was to address the

---

[1] (In 1951) A student tells a reporter, "Robert College taught us about American ideals. Now I try to pass these on to our peasants who are poor, ignorant and opposed to change. In the face of these hurdles, our best weapon is the Americans, good books and good ways." Hasmet Babaoglu, Sabah, 19.1.2023. Hiperlink: https://bit.ly/3RkTX8E

scientific roots of today's political schism, thereby questioning the power of the 600-year-old Ottoman devshirme administration whose rule ended with the People's Democratic Revolution of July 15, 2016.

As my work on the Ottoman state system progressed, I realised that the schism between the central ruling devshirme elite and the ruled-reaya in the periphery encompassed not only history but a wide variety of disciplines. Structure of the central devshirme system, history of Ottoman rural realm, Seljuks, Central Asian steppe state philosophy, nomadic culture, anthropology, sociology, ethnology, psychology, social psychology, political psychology, political science, Islam, Alawite-Sunni relations, Muslim-non-Muslim relations, rebellions, military coups, the Istanbul guild, the agricultural system, elite/folk art, music, literature, Westernization, Tanzimat, the process of evolving into a republic, educational philosophy, Atatürk, Medieval Europe, comparison of the Western and Ottoman political philosophies, and civilisations were the disciplines to be tackled. Furthermore, it is next to impossible to describe a being called Turk. Incomprehensible, unpredictable, and a grey area that drives an outside observer crazy.

Further was the need to search for the reasons for Ottomans lagging behind Europe. As Ottoman victories and conquests stopped and the decline started, the administration could not pay the salaries of janissaries. Hence the need for novel solutions for rational, disciplined budget systematic. Modernisation measures were protested by the janissaries, and the viziers were lynched for such efforts, and such reactions persisted through centuries of vicious cycle.

To summarise, it was a herculean job to research the wide-ranging, multidisciplinary review of Türkiye's historical political schism by one person.

Also, the job of writing a semi-academic book with a reference in every sentence was putting a straitjacket on my brain, getting it into an iron discipline, destroying the human-touch of my message. Mevlana Rumi's famous metaphor is well worth mentioning here: just as "sugar melting in water," like the colours of the art of marbling "ebru", knowledge melts in the brain rather than staying as heterogenous patches side by side in the brain. As the homogenous knowledge builds up in the subconscious, it instinctively spills out of the brain in a spontaneous flow. A flow coming from the subconscious, from the soul, one cannot stop pouring out.

I guess I couldn't quite make it. So I decided to push aside everything, the references of the thousands of pages of books I've read, put aside my English book preparations, and wrote the comprehensive, short Turkish summary for the Turkish audience, the original work of this translation.

As masters paper down their arguments in striking, gripping, persuasive ways and short sentences; for amateurs, references come as lifesavers, and for me, especially with the chapters on psychology.

I wish every line in this short, intense book would introduce something of value to the reader, and lead him/her to a deeper level of reflection. I also look forward to receiving feed backs and reactions to this trial, from the most hostile attacks to the best intended and constructive ones, to further mature my analysis.

As I was writing my book, my most pressing concern was of rejecting my Ottoman heritage as did the early Republic's founders.[2] What if someone who reads my book gets angry at the ruling devshirme and refuses our Ottoman grandfathers like early Republican revolutionaries?

Türkiye, since the early 19th century, has been in an identity crisis. The pendulum, which has been swinging between temporal and spiritual lifestyles for two hundred years, needs a little more time to come to a stand-still, a "sound middle point" so that the chaos in people's minds finds peace and the modern Turkish identity can be established.

Lastly, my words of introduction to my international readers: as we humans are members of the same global family, many other peoples may see their similar problems in the lines of this humble work, and even identify with them. I hope this book could also be useful for them as well as we, the Turks.

---

[2] "Although Atatürk's negative view of the Ottomans is known..." says Halil Inalcık. Yeni Safak Newspaper 3.12.2022, Hyperlink: https://bit.ly/3HEhE8H

CONCEPTS

Reading drafts, some of my friends warned me that my heavy style was fit for the erudite, but not for the laymen. That some of the concepts used in my book could be misunderstood. Hence I put the main concepts in simpler form in the beginning pages.

The book was built on two main pillars.

Firstly, **psychology**: This section discusses the psychology of the lumpen masses in transformation. Masses migrated from villages to the metropols, and in the process of urbanisation, modernisation and secularisation, swiftly lost their millennial values based on religion and tradition. And in need of at least five generations to construct modern secular values, especially ethical ones. Here, the clash is between the urge to cling to the "inherent" historical values, and reformulate them in modernity versus the urge to unconditionally dump everything of heritage and join the band of modernists, with the fear of being ostracised from the ruling, dominant elite.

Secondly, the **classes**: Two classes lived in tension in the Ottoman Empire. In the Platonist sense, the Ruler (centre, devshirme bureaucracy) and the Ruled (periphery, reaya). The history of the tension between these two alienated classes, still continuing in the Republic, forms the second part of our book.[3]

---

[3] The entire Turkish history can be summarized as the center's attempt to control the periphery, in other words, the history of

Bourgeois

The word "bourgeois" used in this book does not denote the term capitalist in the Marxist sense, but "burgher", i.e. "within city walls - civilised - urban nobleman". Referring to a person who has learned manners, protocol and mutual respect over the centuries and whose ethical and aesthetic values have reached a refined level, which we call the late Ottoman "Istanbul Efendisi – Gentleman of İstanbul".

As such qualities have evolved through centuries in Europe and Istanbul, such formation for the lumpen masses may require at least five generations to acquire. We may surmise Türkiye, 90% peasant in the 1920s, passed three generations of urbanisation. It may need two more generations or another forty-plus years for the settlement of modern values and to reach the new "Istanbul Efendisi" in Türkiye.

---

sibling rivalries. We Turks are known for our ability to destroy the state as well as for our ability to establish one. It is the most tragic aspect of our history that it was the Turks who destroyed almost all of the Turkish states we established in history. A central authority dealing with sibling rivalries cannot dominate and control the entire society. Local power groups attempt to revolt whenever they get the opportunity. Double norms for morality and law naturally develop when local powers are so dominant. In this social structure, tribal consciousness takes precedence over common consciousness, causing all kinds of corruption to emerge easily. Erol Göka, Türk Grup Davranışı, Asina Books, Istanbul, 2006, p. 242

Lumpen

Lumpen is a German-based concept made famous by Karl Marx and Friedrich Engels. However, in this book, this concept is not used in the sense of "lumpenproletariat", that is, the poor masses lacking class consciousness in the Marxist sense. Here, a lumpen is a person who quickly, sometimes knowingly and eagerly, loses his rural morals and values (actually, his noblesse) based on religion and tradition distilled over millennia, as he migrates to the metropol from the periphery. The term denotes the rough person, hick, who has not yet internalised the secular morality of the city. Even a college degree cannot give them the ethical and aesthetic refinement, the values which would require generations to evolve.[4]

Devshirme

Basically, best defined in the Mukaddima of Ibn-Khaldoun for former Islamic practices, for the Ottomans, "Devshirme" is the non-Muslim slave soldier/bureaucrat gathered from Balkan families, a practice which was started during the reign of Murad I (15th AD) and became an institution during the reign of Fatih (Sultan Mehmed II The Conqueror). In a narrow sense, it is an institution of approximately one hundred and fifty years between Fatih and Murad III.

---

[4] Our 20th century architecture is a striking example of this bizarre era.

However, for the purpose of our thesis, the concept is used in defining the practice of "alienating" bureaucrats of a five-hundred-year history. That is to say, a devshirme is a young man taken from his village (periphery) and educated at the elite palace college Enderun, and "alienated" from his town and roots. Alienation of a young man from his peasant values, family, even reaching levels of the hatred of his roots and self-hatred. Such alienating education philosophy continues in the Republican curriculum in our day. Simply, the more educated one becomes, the more alienated he is from his roots.

Devshirme and the Sultan were an inalienable duo getting strength from each other. However, when Atatürk abolished the Sultanate, the devshirme body lost its brain. Fluttering headless for another century, by the 21st century, it gave in to the new bureaucrats of provincial heritage, appointed by the politicians of the rising periphery (reaya).

Türkmen

A martial steppe race of Central Asia, having ruled China, India, Persia, Caucasus, Arab lands, North Africa and East Europe, Türkmen is the founding core of both the Seljuk and the Ottoman Empires.

Although Türkmen is the founding core of both the Seljuk and the Ottoman Empires, once they established these states, they were excluded from the administration.

Given their martial spirit, they were assigned the military role of the guardians of these empires. Apart from 150 years of recruitment of janissaries from the Balkans, non-muslim reaya of the six-hundred-year Empire were not permitted to be soldiers. They were assigned crafts and trade.

For our thesis, Türkmen refers to the "reaya - the ruled" in the periphery as a whole. And the theme of our book is based upon the alienation of the Ottoman ruling devshirme class from the founding core Turkmens. The term Turkmen not only denotes the settled ones but also the Yörük, wondering Türkmens, who were constantly forced to settle for tax collection and military recruitment.

∧

With the republican awakening of Anatolia, Turkmens seized power six centuries later and took the state administration from the hands of the devshirme, who were alienated from their origin. Thus, Turkmen goes back to work in the 21st century.

Ataturk

For our thesis, we will examine Mustafa Kemal Atatürk from three perspectives.

The first concern is about the question of whether he is on the side of the devshirme bureaucrat class or on the side of the people.

The clear answer is seen in the speech he gave at the opening of the Turkish Grand National Assembly (TBMM) on March 1, 1922:

"The true owner and master of Türkiye is the peasant who is the actual producer. Indeed, for seven centuries, we have wasted their labour and shed the blood of these people by sending them to different parts of the world, leaving their bones in battlefields. We have denigrated them with insults and humiliation. For seven centuries, we have reduced them to servants with ingratitude squandering their labour, treated them with scorn and derision. We have been thankless, arrogant and oppressive against their self-sacrifice and benevolence. Today, in the presence of these true owners of the homeland, let us take our respectful stance with great shame and respect."

One of the first operations of the leader, who apologised to his peasants, was to abolish the tithe (10% crop tax) despite dire economic conditions and fierce opposition from his assistants.

Ataturk's revolution, perhaps never understood until today, ended the sultanate and left the devshirme, the alienated Ottoman military/civil bureaucrats, headless. Yet the peasants had to wait another Century to topple the experienced, hardened historical ruling class, which Atatürk could not. A belated result in the 21st century was the overthrow of this headless ruling class from its millenial role by the periphery.

Although Atatürk, like the author of this book, was of the historical DEVSHIRME bureaucracy, he was against his class which was alienated from the people. But he was helpless. As the lone star faded, devshirmes, re-starting with their new President, General İsmet İnönü, resumed enjoying their historical privileges until 21st century. Perhaps the psychological and political rift between Atatürk and İnönü near Atatürk's demise had roots in this failure.

"Atatürk knew (with the experiments of Terakkiperver Fırka – Progressive Party and Liberal Fırka – Liberal Party) that the Republican People's Party was the party of the minority in the country. He died despondent and lonely. In general, competing bureaucrats suspect each other are lonely people. Indeed, the person most opposed to M. Kemal near his death was certainly his closest associate - once upon a time".[5]

Our second topic is Atatürk's philosophy. In his famous book, "The Protestant Ethic and the Spirit of Capitalism", Max Weber elaborates on living for the next world versus this world among Catholics and Protestants.[6] As a statesman, Ataturk also was stuck on these two approaches to life. The question of the time. Temporal, or spiritual? He noticed that Christian Europe had developed by passing from a spiritual to a material

---

[5] Idris Kucukomer, Düzenin Yabancılaşması-Batılılaşma, Kapı Publications, Istanbul, 2021, p. 113
[6] Max Weber, The Protestant Ethic and the Spirit of Capitalism

approach to life. [7] And he wanted the same "enlightenment" for his people. The Turk, who had been sleeping for the hereafter for a thousand years, had to wake up to the material world, like Max Weber's Protestants have done.[8] Yet we had no infrastructure! His dream of making his people MATERIALIST - interestingly- was realised by the economic revolutions of two pious Presidents, Turgut Özal and Recep Tayyip Erdoğan.

Our third issue is at least as important as the first two. The issue of legitimacy. Even though nearly a century has passed since his death, Atatürk is still the main "SOURCE OF LEGITIMACY" in Turkish politics.

Although urbanisation, an important base for the middle classes and democratic spirit, has caught momentum, Turkish democracy has not yet reached the maturity of getting power from the people. That's why,

---

[7] Superiority of the West, which accelerated the consumption-production-technology-information cycle with the Industrial Revolution, primarily on the battlefields and the military, was felt by the Ottomans, and that it was necessary to transform the spiritual, mystical, grateful lifestyle into a materialist lifestyle and to implement policies to that end. For most high-ranking politicians, getting rich and owning property became a fixed idea. And all means to such end were permissible. Goka,2006, ibid. page 241

[8] "For Atatürk, Istanbul was 'spiritual' and Ankara was 'temporal'. The secular state could only be established from Ankara. According to Atatürk, Istanbul was a capital that excluded Anatolia. It was impossible to build a national identity from Istanbul". Zafer Toprak, Darwin'den Dersim'e Cumhuriyet ve Antropoloji, Doğan Book, 2012, p. 74

be it military juntas or politicians, aspiring groups for power still feel the need to get their legitimacy from the name of Atatürk, not from the people. As long as political legitimacy is based on the name of Atatürk, Turkish democracy will not feel the need to take its legitimacy from the people; it will not be able to prove its maturity and will be delayed in this regard. In short, the source of political legitimacy will still remain Atatürk, but not the people. Encouragement of the Western world to such anti-democratic urges is based on the wrong premise that Ataturk wanted pro-European values. He was a positivist, yes. But not Europeanist.

15 July 2016 Democracy Day

The Ottoman and Republican juntas could overthrow any government whenever they desired, in the comfort that there would be no grassroots reaction against them. The night of July 15, 2016 was a historical turn. It was the revolution of the millennium, equal, or more tectonic than the French Revolution. People resisted tanks with bare hands, stood up for their elected President for the first time, gave 250 martyrs and more than two thousand wounded. National Congress, Presidential Palace and General Staff Campus were bombed by air force jets. It was the first bloody clash in Republican history. Any junta going against people's will would, from then on, know that it should be ready for a bloody internal war. The millennial practice of palace coups was no longer possible. Grassroots were the new sovereign. On 15 July 2016, Turkish people declared to the world that from now on, they would protect their elected politicians by blood and would not leave them at the mercy of juntas, modern janissaries anymore.

INTRODUCTION

Transformation

Through the eyes of Prof. Zafer Toprak, Türkiye 1927:

"As of March, "Resimli Ay" Magazine would begin to publish the survey results. Headline in the March 1927 issue was: "Turkish youth do not know what they want, what they read, what they worship. Mind of the Turkish youth was in chaos. Turkish youth did not have a common ideal, nor purpose".

Of the three hundred and fifty interviewed, forty responded as they did not believe in anything. For them, there was neither God, nor a prophet. Nor was the Qur'an a holy book. One hundred believed in a God. But it was not the one their teachers were portraying. Some described the Prophet as a mentor, a genius, a great man of his time. These young people did not attach importance to religious upbringing and did not believe in the necessity of religion for society. The remaining two hundred and ten were faithful."[9]

Meaning? Of the 350 students, 40 were atheists, 100 deists, and 210 faithful, about a third of the future bureaucrats to rule Muslims of Türkiye were "Non-

---

[9] Zafer Toprak, Türkiye'de Yeni Hayat - İnkılap ve Travma 1908-1928, Doğan Book, 2019, p. 230

Muslim Turks".[10] In the age of transition from spiritual to temporal, the other part, the faithful, were intimidated and brushed aside from executive posts of the new state.

Temporal was the victor over the spiritual. The Turk, in the millennial sleep for the next world, was to wake up to this world like Weber's Protestant. But the country did not have the infrastructure for such an awakening. Infrastructure of the new materialist lifestyle was to come by the economic revolutions of two pious Presidents, Özal and Erdoğan.

Evolution of Devshirme from the Sword of Islam into the Sword of Materialism

Let us give a cross-section of the Tanzimat (Westernisation) mentality with the "materialist medical students" of 1845, and later during the reign of Sultan Abdulhamid II.

"In 1845 (British traveller Charles) MacFarlane was horrified to see the "materialistic" spirit inculcated by French teachers in students of the College of Military Surgeons".[11]

---

[10] Bureaucrats were trying to impose Western institutions, Western culture and Western lifestyle on the public within the historical Ottoman tradition, and without giving anything to the masses. These were called revolutions. And these last two facts was bringing the bureaucrat-people contradiction to the forefront." Kucukömer, ibid. p. 115

[11] Şerif A.Mardin "The Genesis of Young Ottoman Thought" Pp 213

Zafer Toprak, in his book *"New Life in Turkey 1908-1928"*, says the following about the educated youth of the late Ottoman and early Republican period:

"The old beliefs in their minds were shaken, but not completely destroyed. New ones did not replace those destroyed. The Turkish youth was restless and undecided between the old and the new."[12]

A Century later, Prof. Erol Goka was saying, *"Let's admit it, especially in our big cities, we are floundering in a brutal era that we neither live our traditional lives anymore, nor became modern."*[13]

Let us borrow some more lines from Prof. Toprak's precious work:[14]

"World War I put many old values on question. It was widely believed that the values that had been considered sacred until then and that governed a society, were suddenly meaningless.

The old values were lost, the essence of life was decimated, and they were all destroyed one by one like lifeless dreams. The youth was now waiting for a "new life" he was not prepared for. It was restless, suspicious, and uncertain. New values were needed for the "new life". It was inevitable to destroy old institutions and bring new

---

[12] Toprak, ibid. p. 221
[13] Goka, 2006, ibid. p. 212
[14] Toprak, ibid. p. 221

values to life. Under these conditions, the post-war "youth movement" came to the fore.

The youth began considering the old society's social, economic, religious, familial and moral values as bankrupt. Now the old religious norms, moral values and the family institution had lost the influence that could hold the youth under discipline. The collapse caused by the World War blew up the values of the social institutions of the old generation such as morality, family and religion. The youth was for living the day."

Sevimli Ay Magazine wrote: "What does today's youth want and believe in? It wants everything and believes in nothing. Neither God, religion, nor morality satisfies today's youth. In the eyes of today's youth, Ford is the greatest man in the world, and the greatest strength is money. The most read books are adventure novels." The youth, who turned their faces to the future, was in a general revolt against all old institutions and norms. It disliked the social and economic order, did not believe in religious and moral principles and regarded old lofty aims and ideals as ridiculous mythifications. In short, a great "revolution" was observed in world youth.

The majority of the youth, whose minds were kneaded by science and philosophy, denied the sanctity of religion. The young people no longer liked their elder's world and saw it as their right to reform everything. The most important point in people's behaviour was their approach to morals. They no longer needed such support to strengthen their character. With a clearer description, the religious upbringing, the style based on spiritual values, which had been given up until that time, had failed in guiding the behaviour of the youth to a secure course.

For young people, Henry Ford was now the idol. The real values were those which served hedonism. The greatest revolt of the new generation was against sexual morality. Sexual activities were the most natural relations, and it was against the laws of nature to suppress such relations. The young generation, boys and girls, now rejected the sexual morality of their elders.

As also understood from the survey, the youth believed only in positive sciences. That is, only in material things. Railways, automobiles, cinema, welfare and peace, and the need for a good life inspired the post-war youth into an extremely materialistic lifestyle. The contemporary world of the 20s no longer valued spiritual and psychical things. For the youth, the idea was not to live a spiritual and inner life but to reach the highest level of material peace and welfare. The most sacred thing for youth was money. To become a great man, one had to accumulate a lot of money."

Considering the values of the Muslim Anatolian peasants closed to the world and Istanbul then, the statistics given by the Resimli Ay Magazine of the radically materialist students of 1927 show the grave schism between the early republican ruling elite and the faithful ruled by them. The schism of Ottoman times was indeed continuing. Yet this time religious divide was at the fore front. Remembering the epidemic of materialism among medical students during Tanzimat, 1927 survey shows the epidemic continued with acceleration in the educational philosophy of the early Republic.

The most important feature of the Ottoman and Republican devshirme bureaucracy, as we will frequently emphasise in this book, is that it is disconnected from the values of the people it governs. As stated in this survey, we can clearly see one of the most important indicators of "alienation" and schism in our educational philosophy dating back centuries.

PART ONE

Psychology

Since the subject of our book is the "political schism" that threatens our social peace, the first issue we need to address is the "Human". The "human" who hates himself… And his community.

First, an anecdote from Chicago: During my tenure in Chicago in the 1990s, at a cocktail party, I started a conversation with an American academic who had just returned from Türkiye and asked him about his impressions of our country. He said, "I'll tell you my sincere opinion if it won't upset you," and continued. "Turks don't like each other". Given the atmosphere of schism in Turkish politics of 2023, such an observation seems so innocent.

The most important element underlying the feeling of hatred is undoubtedly the psychology of the society still living in a period of transformation – from peasant life to a metropolitan, modern, Western lifestyle.

The source of many problems is the "feeling of inferiority and the yearning of the peasant new to the city, to be embraced by the modern urban community." Such psychology requires the creation of the "other". And for the educated new modernist peasant, the "other" is his very family and its values left back in the village. From peasant to urban, we may call the interim phase of transformation as "lumpenization process".

Perhaps the most important loss in shifting to a materialist, modern lifestyle are two traditional Turkish Islamic values: "compassion and mercy." In his war to success by any means, young metropolitan modernist youth would not even know what these two words mean. And without these two words, it seems hard to have inner peace, and more, social harmony.

That's why we put the psychology section first.

Our basic question is: What is poisoning the political environment in Türkiye?

Is it our unquestioning, fanatic commitment to the lifestyles and values of the groups we belong to? Namely, religious and secular?

Is it the "conformism" that Nietzsche draws attention to, the cowardice of being excommunicated from the group we belong to?

What are the psychological reasons underlying the bigoted, stubborn loyalties in politics? With which motives is one a Kemalist, secularist, Westernist, modernist, CHP (The Republican People's Party) supporter?

And with which motives is one AKP (Justice and Development Party) supporter, devout, conservative, or else liberal, leftist, pro-sharia etc?

Though I am not a psychologist, and cannot claim to be one, I did a little homework reading the books of

Abraham Harold Maslow, Alain de Botton, Alfred Adler, Carl Gustave Jung, Erol Göka, Erol Güngör, Friedrich Nietzsche, Martha Cottam, Nevzat Tarhan, Nur Vergin, Sigmund Freud and Vamik Volkan. Encouraged by my readings, I made a humble try, daring to discuss the subject of human psychology.

Individual Psychology (Fission)

Can we say two key components constitute human psychology? The first, the desire to be "oneself", to be "me", to be "unique", and to be "different" from others. Let's call it fission i.e. the need for dissociation. Turkish saying goes: "If one does not like himself, he would burst of sorrow."

Let's hear Friedrich Nietzsche: *"At present it belongs to the conception of "greatness" to be noble, to wish to be apart, to be capable of being different, to stand alone, to have to live by personal initiative"*[15]

We want to be ourselves. But who do we want to be? Let's remember the famous 13th Century Turkish sufi Yunus Emre and Socrates. Do we really know who we are, what we desire in life? Some of us go into an identity crisis through a certain awakening. A small, wise group overcomes the crisis and finds a calm soul and peace. Some leave the world without even having an identity crisis, let's call them lazy souls without identity. Some

---

[15] Friedrich Nietzsche "Beyond Good and Evil." section 212, the "The Great Man."

even want to be someone else, spend their lives imitating others, and even think that they are someone other than themselves. Some brag about how many "important acquaintances" they have, trying to cure their weaknesses with the strength of others. Although we are in the age of ChatGPT, some are trying to gain respect by memorising information in an effort to prove how much they know, to their peers. Add to that the exhibitionism unleashed by social media. We have to consider this psychological background in the sociopolitical preferences of the creature we call human.

Abraham Maslow considers "self-esteem" as one of the five most important needs on the scale of human vital needs *(physiological needs, safety needs, belongingness and love needs, self-esteem needs, and self-fulfilment needs)* and emphasises that its absence causes weakness, feelings of inferiority and helplessness.[16]

Alain de Botton says, *"In modern secular societies, a more miserable destiny cannot be imagined than 'being like everyone else'... Mediocre people, those who cannot go beyond the general line of society, the mass of the people and the boring people... However, the main purpose of an intelligent individual is to stand out from the crowd and to stand out from society as much as its abilities allow."*[17]

---

[16] Abraham H. Maslow, A Theory of Human Motivation, [First published January 18, 1943]
[17] Alain De Botton, Statü Endişesi, trans. Ahu Sıla Bayer, Sel Publishing, Istanbul, 2023 [First published in 2004], p. 285

In his works, Friedrich Nietzsche curses the herd spirit and deals with the ideas of difference, loneliness, freedom, and being oneself.

The debate continues as to whether human values and behaviour codes are innate or result from the environment.

In fact, many psychologists and philosophers say that humans can't live outside of society, like many other animals, as we will explain in the "fusion" section. On the other hand, Nietzsche opposes this view, which he calls the "herd spirit", with the thesis of "Ubermensch-Superior Man." He says that psychologically strong people should reject all values and create their own values, follow them, and even surpass themselves. He claims that one can very well live alone and free.

Alfred Adler writes: *"From the standpoint of human's relationship to nature, human is an inadequate creature. Being human entails experiencing inadequacy and making an effort to achieve superiority."*[18] He also notes that this goal manifests itself under the guise of having authority over others and being more powerful and superior to them.

Adler states that at the root of human values and behaviours, there is an inferiority complex arising from helplessness, insecurity and anxiety that starts at the moment of birth, against the power of nature, and that

---

[18] Alfred Adler, İnsanı Tanıma Sanatı, trans. Kamuran Şipal, Sel Publishing, Istanbul, 2022
[İlk yayın tarihi 1934], p. 6

whole life passes in search of the satisfaction of this feeling of inferiority. Furthermore, he asserts that this has reached the point where he hates society, those in power, and even himself. According to Nietzsche, who concurs with Adler, *"This burnout, this self-hatred - all this emanated from it with such strength that it became a new hindrance to it."*[19]

Furthermore, Adler continues, *"We frequently hear from such people that their parents also have an 'aristocratic' character. The tendency to believe that one is different from others, comes from an 'extraordinary' family, is endowed with excellent purpose and emotions, is born with privilege, and is superior to everyone else, is all that can be found behind this empty desire."*[20]

"There is isolation and fragmentation in the nature of modern values that claim to replace our values based on tradition", writes Prof. Hayrettin Karaman about the issue of modern loneliness.[21]

Freud, on the other hand, explains that the individual behaves with the Id (instinctive, primitive, animalistic), Super-Ego (trying to restrain id with concepts such as conscience, and morality) and Ego (arbitrating the conflict between the id and the superego and trying to reconcile them with the realities of life) impulses.

---

[19] Nietzsche, ibid. p. 141
[20] Adler, ibid. p. 107
[21] Hayrettin Karaman, Farklılaşma, parçalanma ve uzlaşma üzerine, Yeni Safak Newspaper, 27.11.2022, Hiperlink: https://bit.ly/3Y64ir8

In other words, a healthy soul is content with itself and seeks to be who it truly is. How common is this in our society, then? The main quest...

Having discussed fission, now let's examine how personal psychological factors like inferiority complex, the need for love and esteem, narcissism, and the desire to dominate, affect a person's social behaviour and political preferences. Hence continue with the disciplines of social psychology and political psychology.

Social Psychology (Fusion)

As the human is a social being, now let us look into social psychology.

Remember Aristotle. His coining the human as "zoon politicon – political animal." Is social interaction of humans a genetic animal instinct? Can humans survive outside a human group?

Alfred Adler starts with the "first fear" that all living things experience at birth. *"A child's understanding of life's challenges is so limited that he is helpless without others to support him and make up for what he lacks. A terrified person, starting with his mother, reaches out his hand to another, try to grab it, pull it, and hold it there forever. That there are no absolutes, and the nearest to the absolute is social life."*[22]

---

[22] Alfred Adler, İnsanı Tanıma Sanatı, trans. Kamuran Şipal, Sel Publishing, Istanbul, 2022

What we can call **fusion**, the need for attraction and recognition, or the desire to be part of a society, is a common nature in general. Except for powerful souls reaching a certain level, like sufis and philosophers, ordinary humans excluded from society pay a very high price. Historical Anatolian dervish orders and religious fraternities used to serve as threads maintaining social group solidarity. Such a mission continues in modernity as economic and social solidarity clubs.

Remember, Maslow listed "security, belonging and love" as social needs. University of Texas Professor Costica Bradatan says biological herd instinct in our brains ensures us a comfortable and trouble-free life, in harmony with society. However, when our minds begin to question the values of the group, and go against our biological motives for fusion, problems arise.[23]

Nietzsche asserts, *"Naturally the strong tend to separate, and the weak tend to unite"*, emphasising the value of isolation for the individual.[24]

According to Charles Mackay, humans are biologically wired with a herd instinct and herd logic. Their survival depends on this instinct, but as they awaken one at a time, they must learn to disperse from the herd. He says that biology and spirit are from

---

[İlk yayın tarihi 1934], p. 6.
[23] Costica Bradatan, The Herd in the Head (article/makale) Hiperlink: https://bit.ly/3RmWizE
[24] Nietzsche, ibid. p.156

different planets, and the only way to achieve spiritual integrity is by breaking away from the crowd. [25]

In this regard, the following lines of sociologist Nur Vergin are noteworthy:[26]

"Hegel asserts that, in addition to wanting to satisfy their own hunger and need for survival, humans also need to fulfil the wishes of other people. A human is a being who desires and requires the company of others. The awareness of one's own distinct human identity depends on being acknowledged by others in this situation, because it is so crucial to the human experience. It's a phenomenon that makes a person human, but it's also a reality that enables it to identify, in essence, with himself as a human being".

Alain de Botton uses the famous, wealthy, well-respected, high judge Ivan Ilyich of Tolstoy's novel as an example of how even powerful human beings long for compassion and a warm embrace:

"Ilyich was most agonised by the lack of affection people showed him. There came moments when he just wanted to be loved and compassionately embraced like a little child after going through so much pain. He yearned for hugs, kisses, and other forms of affection. He desired to receive the same level of attention given to ill children.

---

[25] Bradatan, ibid.
[26] Nur Vergin, Din, Toplum ve Siyasal Sistem, Bağlam Publishing, Istanbul, 2000, p.223

At his advanced age and greying beard, indeed he knew he was a significant official. Alas! He wanted affection."[27]

Alain de Botton also refers to the cruelty of society. *"Individuals without status are treated harshly, their colorful personalities are ignored, and their identities are despised in society. More importantly, having low status ruins their self esteem.* He highlights the modern man's constant worry about falling into a lower social stratus with the following words: *"Confident People do not make fun of those around them. Perhaps snobbishness is motivated by hysterical fear. Deep fear is the source of haughtiness and arrogance."* He advises us to ask the question: *"Is it me or is it my position that matters in society?"*

Given the above views, let's ask: Are our political preferences the results of our conscious choices arising from the fear Nietzsche draws attention to, or the groups we choose by subconscious, spontaneous psychological effects?

Conformism

Conformism is exactly what Nietzsche despises and wants to debunk. Capitulation and conformity to social norms.

"The sick animal called human, which degenerates and shrinks into a herd animal, behaves with a herd

---

[27] De Botton, ibid, p. 225

instinct, and adopts the judgment that society sees as 'good or evil' without scrutiny."[28]

We can define conformism as the "Desire to be a good boy, not causing problems in our community." Anyone who tries to undermine the group's faith is immediately shunned and ostracised. We shall discuss excommunication and its consequences in the next chapter.

Nietzsche illustrates the ease of conformism with the words: *"How the world pleases our hearts, treats us in a friendly way, when we surrender to its will".*[29]

According to Nietzsche, modern culture aims to transform the wild man *"into a more ordinary, more irresponsible, more Chinese, more Christian pet for the sake of a comfortable life."* For him, the creature made *"regular, reliable, uniform"* by severe sanctions and punishments of the society will have arrived at the end of history (not the one in Fukuyama's book).[30]

As the human being was a social creature, let's see what Psychiatrist Prof. Erol Göka wrote in his book "Turkish Group Behavior" on the human need for conformism:

---

[28] Nietzsche, ibid. p.79
[29] Nietzsche, ibid. p. 111
[30] Friedrich Nietzsche, On the Genealogy of Morality, Ed. Keith Ansell-Pearson, trans. Carol Diethe, Cambridge University Publishing, Cambridge, 2006, p.16

"Those who wish to live in a community, must fit in with its present members. These psychological behavioural patterns are very resistant to the flow of history. Individual in such environment, finding it too comfortable to leave, rather than facing his conscience, pretends to submit to the system, hence avoiding his responsibilities."[31]

According to Costica Bradatan, *"Life is empty when you're alone because you're nothing. However, its eruptive, limitless energy fills you once you achieve a meaningful integration with the herd. The pack fills the emptiness you've fallen into, gives you greatness and dignity, gives meaning to your confused existence, and this collective spirit has a very dangerous power. A person's psychology that prevents him from harming a bird when he's by himself, can change in an instant. That person can torch a government building and rob a liquor store because common sense turns into madness, caution into carelessness, and kindness into barbarism."*[32]

In the following section of his article, Bradatan also quotes Elias Canetti:

"The individual caught in the swarm whirlpool is unable to break free from that group spirit. Even a murder that is fervently desired and shared by the herd can be carried out safely if not outright encouraged. People receive joy and dignity from the herd that they cannot receive from family, friends, or the workplace. It

---

[31] Göka, 2006, ibid. p. 39
[32] Bradatan, ibid.

acts as a highly toxic drug-like therapeutic agent on his psyche."

Now, among these academic viewpoints, I would like to insert a memory of my own. My days as a teacher of English language at a high school in Ankara.

It's 1976, a time when terrorism wreaks havoc in the nation. The atmosphere at schools is dominated by the revolutionary Marxist left. Students scroll the corridors with guns in their pockets. I am a "light pinky leftist", I don't engage in politics, the school principal is a rightist from the MHP (Nationalist Movement Party), and I am an adored teacher.

One day, while we were in class, we heard humming outside, and then someone kicked open the classroom door. "Guys, we're taking action, everybody out!" shouted a brat in a parka. Do my pupils adore me? Having that faith, I mustered the courage to tell the bully, "You stop at that door!" I began, and then these words escaped my mouth:

"Dear young people, I'll take a moment:

Think of sheep in a flock. And a shepherd dog disciplining them. Above the dog, a shepherd, above the shepherd, an attendant, then the owner whom the flock never sees.

Here's your homework:

Choose which one you want to be in your life.

Yet... Remember the ancient proverb.
One who leaves the herd is the prey of the wolf.
Choice is yours.

I vividly recall how my students left the classroom with ashamed faces.

My frank talk in class was probably inspired by Nietzsche's idea of conformism. Who knows?

We can apply conformist behaviour to two dominant groups in Turkey. The conservative Islamists, and the Kemalist/positivist secularists. Both groups are very easy to enter and exit. Being a lumpen is sufficient.

Entering these groups doesn't demand any mental effort. An intellectual, curious mind finds it extremely difficult to fit in with these groups. The foundations of both are memorisation and faith.

A lumpen, primary school dropout woman can be respected among her community if she gets rich, dyes her hair blonde, dons a two-piece formal black suit, and declares, "I am a Kemalist." She is promptly regarded as modern, progressive and Western.

For the Islamist class, a headscarf is the code. On both sides, be it religious or secular moral values, what matters is loyalty to the groups. Given ladies' dress codes are more illustrative, I have given an example of it. Men's world is even more complex. "Lifestyle" is the keyword.

Lifestyle is an existential battleground. Western nations -particularly the USA- have elevated their lifestyle to the level of religion. And extremely sensitive in this regard. They try to impose their way of life on non-Western nations with fanatical missionary zeal. They want to see Westernised cadres in positions of authority in weaker countries. They view rulers not assimilated into Western lifestyle and world outlook, as threats to their global order and want to remove them from power. Briefly, "lifestyle" is the neo-imperialist instrument for the interests of the West.

The majority of elites from underdeveloped nations happily leave their traditions and conform to the Western way of life. And conformism in the cosmopolitan global hierarchy brings global class solidarity. They receive meagre benefits from Westerners who refer to them as "our useful idiots".

Beyond psychological gratification, conformism returns in the form of economic welfare and social status. Examples of unethical commercial practices include secular, Westernised corporations running advertisements on November 10th, mourning Atatürk's death anniversary, traditional ones using religion to promote celebrations on religious holy days, etc.

The innocent game begins in childhood. When the peasant kid selling Quran in the village for one lira, moves to the metropol, he discovers that the Quran sale does not generate any revenue, and that Atatürk's portraits, busts, and books replace Quran as ten times more profitable commercial material. Now a lumpen in transition, the kid quickly realises the need to change his religion/tradition-based lifestyle into a secular/materialist lifestyle to make a living. The kid grows up and sells Atatürk's books for thousands of liras to lumpens like himself.

Then the social atmosphere starts changing. Religious, traditional masses of the periphery start marching towards the metropols. 90% peasant Türkiye of 1920s, becomes 93% urban in 2020s. Defiant, they resist assimilation into Western values, unlike their predecessors, who came in absorbable numbers before. Time goes on, now the kids see that being Islamist also brings social statute and material gains in the metropol. As there was the millennial ruling elite before, now it was being challenged by the newcomers from the periphery.

Modern/Conservative "lifestyle" conflict and cultural alienation of the two groups from one another shall be covered in more detail later. Just to note, despite what might seem to be a war of pious versus secular, the severe conflict born out of the tectonic demographic shift is not a war of Islamist versus Kemalist. As late Prof. Idris Kucukomer has pointed out, this conflict is not one between faiths. It is class warfare in the Marxist sense. It is the continuation of the historical schism between the ruling central Devshirme class versus Reaya of the periphery, this time the periphery claiming the state from the devshirme, the millennial alienated class, and the founding Turkmen. Now, we see the start of a bitter challenge forcing the masses to choose their sides and strictly conform to them.

Social Exclusion (excommunication)

Herd morality, according to Nietzsche, was the social group conditioning, defining what is right and wrong. And the blind instinct to obey this conditioning, was conformism.

Because they were lazy, desperate, or wanted to stay out of trouble, most people chose conformity in society. And the übermensch of Nietzsche, the superior man, who questioned and rejected this conditioning, faced the threat of excommunication or attack from the herd.

Psychiatrist Prof. Nevzat Tarhan highlights social stigmatisation:

"Social stigmatisation or labelling is defined as the determination of a person's social status, including the placement of that person in a particular cultural pattern and the establishment of that pattern's norms. It is necessary to first create prejudice to categorise people. Stigma is used to control, categorise, diminish, or elevate certain cultural subgroups."

"Colloquial fashion among the devshirmes, the phrase 'yurdum insanı - my peasants' is being used to dehumanise a particular cultural group. The consumption of lahmacun (a traditional minced meat pizza), Turkish folk music, and arabesk (music of the underdog) are all considered to be manifestations of primitive culture. To be modern, these must be given up. Western music is considered to be of modern taste, same understanding is also reflected in clothing. Even how food is eaten with the right and left hands is defined by

Western culture. Under cultural definition, all the above was summed up as modernity. "[33]

Let's give an ear to the late Prof. Erol Güngör now:

"The judgment of others is one of the severest intimidations that makes us cautious about moral behaviour. Nobody can help but consider what other people are thinking when engaging in unethical behaviour. One social psychologist asserts that our personalities are shaped by what other people want to see in us. Although not entirely accurate, this statement still expresses a profound truth."

"To fall out of favour, lose reputation and to gain notoriety, to be despised, reprimanded and especially to be mocked scares us. The impact of public opinion is more noticeable in smaller communities. Any villager's immoral behaviour quickly spreads to the entire village community, such person would instantly lose all of his friends. People who find themselves in such situation leave and move into cities."[34]

Costica Bradatan says that the society will not advance unless we eradicate the herd mentality, namely peer pressure from the community, partisanship, bigotry, fashion, intellectual imitation, and other kinds of –isms.[35]

---

[33] Nevzat Tarhan, Toplum Psikolojisi ve Empati, Sosyal Şizofreniden Toplumsal Empatiye,
TİMAŞ Publishing, Istanbul, 2019, p. 42-48
[34] Erol Güngör, Ahlâk Psikolojisi ve Sosyal Ahlâk, YER-SU Publishing, Istanbul, 2021, p. 148
[35] Bradatan, ibid.

Given the lines above, it is clear that where there is a high degree of conformism, herd instinct, and fear of rejection, a society cannot advance. And that extraordinary individuals cannot emerge in a society. Is the 'mystery' of our lagging behind for centuries hidden here?

Being respected and loved is a fundamental human goal in every era of history and region of the world. Excommunication by the Vatican during the Middle Ages had a psychological impact that was worse than death. It is interesting to note that, in excommunicating beliefs and practices that run counter to their own ideologies, modern secularist priests are equally as effective as inquisition priests in their accusations.

Sure, secularists don't set people on fire. However, they do not grant their adversaries the freedom to coexist in secular communities. This is especially so for the educated and well-to-do people who are accused by their peers of bigotry/regressiveness. Severe social and psychological destruction awaits them. Under such pressure, wannabe lumpens, who have not yet established a strong personality, are forced to Nietzsche's conformism.

Effects and destruction of excommunication on human psychology have been researched by the Universities of Georgia and San Diego. The following are the effects of social exclusion, per scientific research findings published in the journal Social Neuroscience:

- It interferes with the brain's normal function,

- Makes it challenging to make correct decisions,

- Leads to learning challenges,

- Leads to behavioural disorders,

- Inducing loss of willpower,

- Escapism i.e. alcoholism,

- Professional and academic failure,

- Incites hostility...

How many of Nietzsche's übermensch (superior men) can endure these scourges? How many people would dare to drop out of their comfort zone? Imagine one who takes action against his Kemalist or Islamist group and dissociates from it. It is practically a social suicide.

Noting the social foundation of human psychology, now let us get into the specifics.

There are moral priests in every age and community who terrorise, particularly the elite. And Nietzsche's conformists are those who have the ability to join the elite class in a society. Self-interest and laziness of the mind are crucial factors here. They lose their ability to think critically about the truths and taboos that Nietzsche refers to as "herd morality." Like in Orwell's 1984, if they have doubts, the "auto-control" mechanism in their brains turns them into fervent upholders of group ideals.

We can observe this fanatic loyalty more in highly educated, yet unpolished, lowly cultured lumpens trying to join the upper echelons of the community.

Remember the Ottoman proverb: "Bir sonradan görme, bir de gavurdan dönme - Beware of the new money, and the zealous new convert to Islam."

Fashion of modernity entered the Ottoman Empire in the 19th century, what we call the age of Tanzimat (Renewal - Reorganisation). Aficionados of fashion were the Ottoman intelligentsia called Young Turks, aspiring to the French lifestyle. They stood up for the materialist, secularist, and Westernist way of life. We call their descendants "White Turks" today. To strengthen their cause, they use Atatürk as a tool against the traditional periphery. As we already said, the most fervent members of this group are those who are the least eligible to join and are in fear of being kicked out of the modernist community and pushed back to their underdog community, what we call the Black Turks.

The early 21st century takes us into a new social formation. The massive, tectonic demographic shift to metropols enriched, educated and encouraged peasants to retain their traditional values. Hence they were not intimated by modernists, rather, started challenging what they called the metropolitan, cosmopolitan "Western Clones."

We may call the new burghers as the "Pious Bourgeois." Emerging new elite.

A new elite that competes with the establishment. They are like the pious Protestant merchants of Weber.[36] They are swiftly modernising, getting rich, bolstered by political power, in much stronger solidarity than the former elite. As such, they can discipline their new class, with the cane of excommunication too.

Before we wrap up our discussion on conformism, let us see the following passages about Turks who emigrated to Western countries:

"Another regressive reaction in the early migration phase, is the self-hatred and over-idealisation of the new home. The nation left behind is denigrated as individual efforts are made to achieve a high social position at new land by working hard.

These retrograde reactions are more prevalent among people coming from Westernised metropols of their home countries. To cope with the negative image of the immigrant in their new land, they do their best to assimilate and identify with their hosts. And try to cut their relations especially with their lower class nationals.

---

[36] Max Weber, The Protestant Ethic and the Spirit of Capitalism, p. 121

However, these efforts mostly go vain, the aspiring immigrant painfully realises that no matter what he does, he will never be one of his hosts."[37]

Extraordinariness

SAPERE AUDE (Dare to know!)

Prof. Costica Bradatan tells us that Western philosophy was based on *"An eccentric, Socrates, whose intellectual sport was mocking the herd. And that he paid for his social defiance and nonconformity with death penalty. And that extraordinary behaviour calls for eccentricity, bravery, defiance, arrogance, doubt, and resistance on the one hand, yet it also draws regret and, in the end, revenge."*[38]

He quotes André Gide, who also says that a great artist must be a nonconformist and a person **who rows against the current of his time**; an unconventional writer, philosopher or artist should not only conflict with the values of society, but also its rituals and ceremonies. Conflicting with the priests of the system, he should risk being marginalised and excommunicated. (Should we pause here and ask if we have such courage)?

The brave should also beware that few will succeed and that the intellectual establishment will prevail in

---

[37] Alper Hasanoğlu, Bir Terapistin Arka Bahçesi, Remzi Publishing, Istanbul, 2009, p.143-145
[38] Bradatan, ibid.

most conflicts. And if they succeed, their ideas will be absorbed, normalised, then perverted, and, at best, transformed into academic subjects. (Can anything better explain how Atatürk was betrayed?)

Prof Bradatan lastly draws attention to his profession, the American Academia, saying, *"In academia, knowledge is cultivated for the purpose of conformity and to increase our power over others, not to be dissenting."*

Political Psychology

Let us start this section with a famous quote from the late Prof. Idris Kucukomer:

"Right is Left, Left is Right in Türkiye"

I go a step further and assert:

Justice and Development Party, AKP of President Erdoğan...
Is the people's Republican, progressive Party in Türkiye.

And People's Republican Party CHP
Is the conservative Ottomanist Party.

Given that People's Republican Party CHP is the extension of the Ottoman devshirme bureaucrats, and which still shows hesitant, defensive, reactive reflexes of a dying Empire, such is a natural definition.

The most interesting anomaly is: CHP thinks it is Republican and against Ottoman. Yet it definitely is the representative of the military and civilian ruling elite of our day in Ottoman Devshirme tradition. No doubt. They indeed show hesitation and reaction to anything novel. Their life approach hails from the Ottoman devshirme word "istemezük – we oppose", a reaction to reformers seeing them as ones to rock the boat of stability, the Asian mentality that left the Empire centuries behind a rising Europe. And again, interestingly, AKP accepts them as Republicans, not Ottomanists. And itself as the successor of the Ottoman system. What a disorientation…

AKP is the representative of the awakening vibrant periphery, breaking the chains of Ottoman reaya, the ruled peasant class, eager to pick the gains of the Republic Atatürk gave them. So, unknowingly, toppling the Ottoman ruling elite bureaucracy, AKP falls into the Republican wing of the Turkish political spectrum. Interestingly, just like their opposite CHP, they are not aware of their natural identity, which locates them in the Republican wing of politics against the Ottomanist CHP. One wonders when both wake up to their real identities.

World intelligentsia also shares this cross-eyed schism about the Turkish political spectrum. It is necessary to look into the psychology that underlies this perplexity.

Having discussed the individual and social psychology as well as the sub-branches like conformism, exclusion, and extraordinariness, let us now look at the main topic of our book, which is how this psychological background influences people's actual political decisions.

My guides for this section were the books of Erol Goka, Kaan Arslanoğlu, and Martha Cottam.

As the name implies, political psychology is a field that combines political science and psychology. It's the field of study that looks at how psychology influences political ideas, choices, and actions of both rulers and subjects, as well as how much genetics, environment, emotion, and reason play a part in it.

Political and psychological elements such as our social identity, perception, self, values, conformism, behaviour, social behaviour patterns, emotions, motivation, race, nationalism, voting, ethnicity, genocide, war, leadership, persuasion, faith, excommunication, the herd subconscious, the role of the media, marginalisation, stereotypes, motivation, ego, etc.

Let's listen to Erol Goka first:

"The history of Türkiye is one of the never-ending sibling quarrels."

"Just as they do today, Turkish communities of old times were split up into groups or segments identifying under certain symbols. Within these groups, one can observe members of every social class. The symbols of these groups, such as the flag, Atatürk, religion, Turkishness, westernisation, and secularism, which are frequently used in political discourse today, are a continuation of our society's historical memory. An attack on symbols is interpreted as an attack on people's identities because each segment's symbols serve as social representational tools and are crucial in the development of social identity. In contrast to class conflicts in the West, which are more realistic and involve negotiation and, ultimately, compromise, the struggle for symbols in our segmented society is more grave. And because they occur on an emotional level, segment conflicts centred on symbols are harder to resolve in terms of identity and personality."

"There is currently no solution for this segmented structure. To the point where one social group outweighs the other, different social groups engage in constant sibling rivalry without resorting to a final, widespread use of force. Because they are aware—consciously or not— that if the issue is to be resolved violently, it will be necessary to obliterate the rest of Turkish society in order to triumph in the end. Therefore, they have only one chance left: Cooperating with foreign powers against the

other segment, or allied against foreign powers only before the exact moment of disintegration."[39]

Let's now attempt to explain the topic with subtitles.

Why Do People Make Politics?

As you may recall, Aristotle referred to the human as "zoon politicon" or the political animal. Politics will always exist where there is society. Force must be used in politics. The hierarchy starts where there is power. Remembering Plato, the rulers and the ruled are separated in the hierarchy. And when people actively engage in politics, a variety of motivations, including the desire for power, interest, lofty ideals, social superiority, and prestige, come into play.

Political Preference

Leaving mission parties aside, why does someone choose right or left? What psychological, socio-psychological, or biological factors play a role in this?

"Why Does One Become Right-wing?"

Let's discuss how Leftist writer and psychiatrist Kaan Arslanoğlu sees the right in his own words:

---

[39] Göka, 2006, ibid. P. 247-249

"As is to be expected, right-wing individuals tend to be questioning and rebellious in other areas of their personal relationships but are underdeveloped or nonexistent when it comes to social and political issues. They have a strong sense of loyalty to the majority, the conventional, and the past.

Compared to leftists, feelings of personal obedience to authority (in a culturally abstract sense) are stronger. They are more traditional and fear innovations and transformations. Their outlook does not question traditional morality and gives little room for individual initiative. They support keeping things as they are.

They rely on conventional forces, the elders, or the belief that God will assist them in some way to solve problems, even when they become grave. They are anchored by convictions rather than logic. They don't expect people or societies to change all that much; all they need to do is find their inner strength or seek refuge in God, and goodness will follow.

The right works to preserve society, while the left aims to transform people. These are the fundamental inherited tendencies. Because of this, being right-wing is simple. Because of his high level of maturity, man has a natural tendency to be right-wing in the absence of cultural and environmental influences. This is actually what we see.

Being right-wing is strongly influenced by the environment. Family comes first when environmental factors are the agenda... It is necessary to be a responsible citizen who abides by established moral principles and laws, as well as to adopt cultural values that will enable one to sacrifice himself for the benefit of society.

Almost all of these are nothing more than right-wing propaganda that has been amplified since the early years of childhood. If a person's natural tendency is to resist change and uphold the status quo, then his right-wing tendencies are strengthened by the general conservative education, propaganda, and environment. Even though this is the general situation, we frequently come across circumstances that are contrary to what we have described due to both genetic and environmental factors."[40]

Evaluating the preceding words, we see how complex Turkish psychology is; we can apply political conservatism to the metropolitan CHP elite, while applying social conservatism to the grassroots periphery of Turkey.

Let's now see what our MD says about his fellow leftists.

"Why Does One Become Left-wing?"

"In this case, as well, genetic factors predominate. Even if a person is raised in a traditional, ultra-religious family, he can still become leftist if his genetic predispositions are strong enough.

---

[40] Kaan Arslanoğlu, Politik Psikiyatri/Yanılmanın Gerçekliği, İthaki Publishing, 2005, p. 95

...Some characteristics of personality, temperament, and thought processes, which are visible as early as infancy, exhibit a genetic tendency to the left.

First off, it should be noted that terms like right-wing and left-wing are no longer as distinct as they once were. In the last twenty or thirty years, the right hasn't lost much of its influence, but the left has suffered greatly. Therefore the right sneaked into the left.

And the left has never been able to be the ideal left in Türkiye. In other words, it has never been able to embrace the labor, the human and enlightenment. It could never implement democratic participation within itself and could not break up from conservatism.

Trying to break its chains from conservatism, it shifted to liberalism and beyond it to the right wing. The fact that a left-wing party today has right-wing and bigoted conservative attitudes is therefore no longer surprising. Still yet, the distinguishing characteristics that make it possible to separate right and left wing people from one another in terms of ideas, although blurred, can still be figured out.

Left for a leftist still means supporting labour, the underprivileged, and the oppressed. In order to practice leftism, one must stand up for human equality and oppose policies and circumstances that do so. No matter their social or economic standing, leftists are those who care more about the oppressed and the poor. They place more emphasis on social justice and equality. Of course, these are not the only genetic factors determining leftism.

The rightists may also harbour compassion and pity for the underprivileged. The characteristics of being genetically opposed to and different from the current trend determines leftism.

Alevis in Türkiye are generally leftists, similar formations exist in Ireland and many other countries. Due to their sectarian traits, their leftism is a leftism of social acceptance, establishing an identity.. They might not understand what it means to be truly rebellious, to question authority, or to be opposed to conventional wisdom. People who turn to leftism due to their environment are groups that harbour negative feelings toward nationalism for a variety of reasons and who also react negatively to dominant religious tendencies."[41]

This is what our psychiatrist, a physician who positions himself on the left, writes. Consider which of the aforementioned traits best describe the Anatolian Turks, who are fighting for change, and which ones best describe our outmoded bureaucracy.

Idris Kucukomer holds a different perspective, parallel to what we said in the beginning lines in political psychiatry: *"The vast majority of Islamist people seen on the right wing are Türkiye's progressives. Their social and economic demands, which are flexible to growth, development, and transformation, are what give them this quality. These goals foster the forces of production,*

---

[41] Arslanoğlu, ibid. p. 99

undermine society's rigid power structure, and promote pluralism."[42]

We now discuss the Modernists and Conservatives.

Modernists

Dilek İmancer says, *"Every modernisation is the outcome of the interaction between tradition and innovation"*. What if we defined Turkish modernisation as the "Muslim urban population's synthesis of its classical tradition and Western modern culture"?

And İdris Küçükömer: *"The Orientalist-Islamist movement is one of the two main currents that have aimed to save the Ottoman society by directing it in the last hundred years. The other is the westernmost-secular movement. This last trend is the so-called and permanent antithesis of the Islamist current in historical development. The important aspect of the Westernist current is that, it appears as a current that prevents the emergence of a real thesis."*

So, according to Prof. Küçükömer, two prevailing theses in Türkiye are the Islamist and the Western, and that "Westernist current" prevents the emergence of a real synthesis. And this is what has happened in the last hundred years. A serious barrier to democratic evolution. Historical social engineering did not succeed in Türkiye. Since 1876, traditionally, 75 percent of the population

---

[42] Kucukomer, ibid. p. 7

has always voted for the rightists and only 25 percent for modernists. The ratio is still the same in 2023.

Why do people become Kemalists?

Unlike in feudal Europe, Ottomans did not have aristocracy to serve as an example to the populace and inspire imitation and emulation to aspirants. Instead, the devshirme bureaucrat ruling class gave its manners, protocol and lifestyle as a guide to those reaya who moved from villages to Istanbul.

The trend continued with the Republic. Especially the rural "war rich" merchants of the early Republican period looked at the bureaucrats for imitation, who, in the 1920s and 30s, were the only literate, quasi-westernised ones.

At this point, socioeconomic factors guided social psychology. A millennial morality based on religion and tradition was rapidly eroding as people moved from villages to cities. Values of the agricultural society, which have been passed down for thousands of years, primarily based on religion and tradition, were quickly vanishing during this transformation into lumpenization. Peasants were waking up to the materialism of this world from a millennial slumber living for the next world. Peasant, indifferent towards worldly goods, was swiftly succumbing to materialism's grasp.[43]

---

[43] Max Weber, The Protestant Ethic and the Spirit of Capitalism, p. 118

The millennial awakening of Muslim Turks from living for the next world to living for this materialist world was different from the Christian awakening of enlightenment. Reaya were too late in transformation, and when they woke up, they started attacking the material goods of this world in greed. Ready to sacrifice anything for the material goods of this world, and now. The genie was out of the bottle, and nothing could stop them. As Europe started relaxing with full stomachs and European civilisation tired, Turks were starting their war for the resources of this world.

Early Republicans were the champions of welcoming materialism the West imposed on Türkiye. Turkish elite happily, and enthusiastically welcomed the positivist cultural and economic imposition, and the urge reached manic proportions in the 21st Century.

Was this what the West wanted? Removing Marx's opium of religion away from the peasants of the world? And the unintended consequences of creating rivals to its own welfare? Should we blame Western capitalism for imposing materialism on the world? Or should Western masses protest such a policy of shooting themselves in the heel?

How about the dilemma of the crusader spirit of eradicating "barbaric" Islam from the face of the earth? Versus making Turks the most fanatic materialists of the world, working with sweat and blood to surpass the West for the resources of THIS world?

As for secular morals, the West developed them, and gradually digested them through centuries. Turkish transformation from village to the metropol is so swift, and the traditional morals evaporate so quickly that Turks have to build their own modernity and secular values in a much shorter time. And the estimate is that it would take at least five generations for the formation of a new, secular code of ethics. Taking the 1960s as the starting point, we may say we need two more generations meaning perhaps another forty years, for the new secular urban values to settle down.

Back to the new merchants and interests of the uneducated tradesmen, who were trying to be successful – they were required to be in harmony with the "ideology and lifestyle" of the bureaucracy, which was their only patron and benefactor in a non-economy. The representative of this deal was CHP. It became a gentry-bureaucrat party. And the "state fed nouveau rich" of the early Republic gradually evolved to be today's big business. This is the reason why they still vote for the CHP, which represents their class. In short, when viewed from the perspective of history and the lens of Prof İdris Küçükömer, CHP became the party of the bureaucrat-capital coalition, neither of the left, nor of the underprivileged – both in terms of culture and economy.

Let us remember the culture of devshirme. The state took the peasant child and alienated him from his origin, making him a "Statesman." With Tanzimat and the consequent Republic, class alienation became much more radical with Westernization.

When the sharp-minded merchant coming from the village to the city realises that the easiest way to get rich in a bankrupt country is to stick to the state for business success, he decides to synchronise his ideology, lifestyle and commercial interests with that of the ruling bureaucratic elite.

Perhaps due to Christian teaching, the greatest evolution of Western Civilisation was its taming the Western man into a global hierarchical discipline. Every Western nation knows its level in the global hierarchy and accepts it. Whereas Islamic teaching is individualistic, unlike papal hierarchy, it has no central authority of faith. Add to it the historical Turkic unruly character, and what you get is a nation having trouble adapting to its scala in the global hierarchy of our day. The best example of this is the foreign policy of Erdoğan of the rising Republic.

Yet business is a different case. Capitalist merchant mentality would sacrifice any value for material success, including toeing the line of global hierarchy. That is what happened in the West. "Homo consumens" was made a coward, afraid of losing his job and everything material he gained in life. The same trend is working in Turkish business life. As the business expands, it leaves the countryside and evolves into Istanbul's big capital. Its continuation is global trade, meaning cooperation with global cosmopolitan capital, synching its interests with the West, entering global hierarchical discipline, hence, in late Attila İlhan's words, making the merchant-bureaucrat duo the economic and cultural compradors of the West.

The alliance of soldiers, bureaucrats and gentry, which started in the early Republican period and was represented by the CHP, continues until the 21st century. The small provincial pious merchants rejecting Western modernity and alienation could only dream of being the local dealers of the great Istanbul capital in Anatolia. Peasant flow to metropols of about 1920s to 1980s was rather slow, and the city could assimilate the newcomers to its modernist culture. With late President Özal's economic reforms, the flow to the cities accelerated and the new rush was in such great numbers that elite culture started faltering in assimilating the newcomers.

The woman in hijab coming from Anatolia was no longer accepting work as the toilet cleaner of the office. Without removing her headscarf, she wanted to be an ambassador, a general, a doctor, professor, and politican, all she could be in a democratic society. (And she got all she wanted in Erdoğan's rule). She moved from the slum to the high society districts of Istanbul.

Now the conditions have matured and two rival groups have formed. One is the capital of Istanbul, represented by the CHP and backed by the military-civilian bureaucracy and Western powers, and the other is the Anatolian capital, represented by the AKP, which wants to preserve its historical traditions. Western allies of the elite will distort this class war between the two capitalist groups as a religious-secularist ideology fight. The West vehemently wants its clones educated in

Western schools, at the helm, to preserve its interests in Türkiye. Local values are a threat to the West. Its unruly, untameable representatives should be prevented from the government by any means. Cadres other than the Westernised ones were considered hostile to the West.

To repeat İdris Kucukomer: *"The Orientalist-Islamist movement is one of the two main currents that have aimed to save the Ottoman society by directing it in the last hundred years. The other is the westernmost-secular movement. This last trend is the so-called and permanent antithesis of the Islamist current in historical development. The important aspect of the Westernist current is that it appears as a current that prevents the emergence of a real thesis."*[44]

The Tanzimat cadres hoped that the Ottomans would be "forgiven" by the Great Powers if they became "Western, Westernist." The junta generals of the Republic, who came from the modernist tradition, were in the same fear. For this reason, they tried to prevent parties representing local values from coming to power for a long time.

Peasants isolated from the world were unaware of the West's negative thoughts about themselves. Look what Prof Hilmi Yavuz says in the History of Europeans: Toynbee wrote: *"We are right to belittle Turkey. Why should we respect those who imitate us? I respect only those who can contribute to my civilisation."*[45]

---

[44] Kucukomer, ibid. p.13
[45] Hilmi Yavuz, Alafrangalığın Tarihi - Geleneğin Tasfiyesi ya da Yeniden Üretilmesi, TIMAS Publishing, 2010, p. 163

Yet, the West is the very civilisation that prevents the evolution of an Islamic democratic environment. Just like Weber's Protestants' gradual, healthy evolution, through a natural process into Christian Democrats, Muslim peoples also want to hold grasp of their own destiny. They want to control their rulers that work for the interests of Western imperialism. As we said, elite military and civilian cadres in Muslim countries, educated in Western schools or Western curricula in Muslim education systems, are the choice of the West to work with. All the rest, educated in Islamic or traditional local mindsets, are seen as a threat, and they must be toppled and replaced by Westernist generals or their obedient civilian cadres to make them seem more democratic than autocratic. To sum up, the West does not let Islamist parties mature into democratic Muslim parties like Christian democrats in the West. Simply, the West is the enemy of democracy in Islamic countries.

Let's not forget that the biggest enemy of imperialism is the democratic society that bravely seeks its rights, protects its state and does not let itself be exploited.

Now we can further deal with interests. It is natural for parties to organise for the interests of their constituents. And at an advanced stage, it is natural for the rural and traditional masses to see their interests in the AKP, while high bureaucracy, Istanbul's big capital and high society vote for the CHP.

How about the rest? The mesmerising, unnatural, confusing, challenging question is:

How come the twenty per cent of the lumpen masses, the historically oppressed, hopeless, uneducated, underprivileged (including Kurds and Alevis), vote for the CHP, the very representative of the historical devshirme, now the "Westernist" high bureaucracy which oppressed them for centuries?

This question is the heart of the book in your hand.

At this point, I think it is necessary to engage individual and social psychology. As against the great majority of the conservative Turkish population, only about 25% vote for CHP, which claims to represent the left (the greatest joke of the Republic in Türkiye. How European socialists embrace them as a socialist partner is the second great joke.)

The reason? "Learned helplessness." Remember Nietzsche's conformism? These hopeless do not or cannot afford to oppose their elite oppressors and fight to overthrow them. And they choose to join the class of oppressors. They abandon their families, aunts, uncles and their values left behind in the countryside and cling to the estranged devshirme in the metropol. The spectacular slogan, the carrot, is so very attractive: Ataturk, Kemalism, progressiveness, modernity, Western lifestyle.

The child of the Yörük Turkmen, who was crushed for a thousand years, now the modern city youth rejects his past. He doesn't want to remember his heritage. Add to this the fear of excommunication in the lumpen groups of athletes, singers and soap opera artists. They have a point. Let's also think about adolescent university students who have not yet developed enough self-confidence.

Take Atatürk's mausoleum: One must go into one minute of silence as learned from the Christian tradition of military attention accompanied by a trumpet sound. For Muslims, no matter what it stands for, it is a Muslim graveyard, and a Muslim prays "Fatiha" with open hands to Allah. Now the hypocrisy is: In the past, the soldier interrupted anyone praying with open hands, forcing him to military attention. Today no official enforcement, fear of guardian generals is gone. Yet a greater fear reigns. If not fear of excommunication, what is the basis of the hypocrisy of military attention, yet whispering prayers inside?

We defined the lumpenisation of the peasant as his transition phase from the village into the metropolitan lifestyle. Psychologically, a peasant aspiring to join the metropolitan bourgeois would be most eager to deny his past. He is now scared to be called "the peasant" among the city dwellers. He becomes a fanatic anti-peasant, the new devshirme candidate. He is unaware of the fact that the time-proven millennial values of his peasant ancestors are even nobler than the modern values he is aspiring to.

As feudals of Europe and other communities had nobility, Ottomans neither had aristocrats nor nobility at the ruling level. For the periphery, there was an equal society with certain privileges of Muslims over non-Muslims. Yet no nobility. Halil Inalcık's words: "Let alone your grandfather's, even your father's grave remains unknown". Hence to talk of nobility is an absurdity for a Turk.

Jump to modernity, settlement in the 21st century, and the lumpen seeking noble roots. It is at this point that the inferiority complex of today's lumpen society becomes striking. Inventing "Pasha Grandfather" heritages,[46] walls decorated with rusty swords from flea markets, seeking modernisation by changing the family name... These are deep psychological issues that require academic analysis.

Let's listen to Adler. *"... We often hear from the mouths of such people that their parents also have such an 'aristocratic' character. However, behind this empty desire lies nothing but the tendency to feel like a person who is not like others, comes from an 'extraordinary' family, is endowed with excellent purpose and emotions, is born with a privilege, and is superior to everyone else."*[47]

As Prof İlber Ortaylı said, it is the inferiority complex of *"being the grandchildren of peasants who used the same oxcart and plough from the times of Hittites with two million malaria, one million syphilis, three million trachomata, millions of tuberculosis, typhus, typhoid,*

---

[46] "Acı çeken paşazade... Babası paşaysa babasının dedesi çoban!". Orhan Pamuk, Cevdet
Bey ve Oğulları, Iletisim Publishing, Istanbul, 2012, p. 255
[47] Adler, ibid. p. 107

louse suffering peasants whose average life expectancy was forty years,".[48]

As Atatürk wrote to his companion İnönü, we are the offspring of a collapsed peasant society. How come two clashing worldviews are born of the same root? What causes identity diversion? In other words, why does the majority of the population adhere to Anatolian traditional values while the minority adheres to Western lifestyle, culture, and cosmopolitan values and marginalise the former? Take the example of a poor boy of the early Republic from a remote Muslim village in Anatolia, walking a mile with bare feet to school. How does the son of this poor peasant become the pork-eating champion of high society in Istanbul? Just one generation! Academic research is needed to study this swift, one-generation transformation.

Grievances of two towering Muslim non-conformists of the early Republic against Western morals and value systems imposed by the early republican rulers:

---

[48] American economist Max Weston Thornburg also states the following observation in his research titled "Turkey: An Economic Appraisal", which he wrote in 1949 Turkey: "Four-fifths of Turks live in villages and are engaged in agriculture. 40,000 villages have remained virtually unchanged for a thousand years. In these villages, one sees pepole using wheeled oxcart and the ancient plow, which the Sumerians painted in 3000 BC. Cavit Orhan Tütengil, 100 Soruda - Kırsal Türkiye'nin Yapısı ve Sorunları, Gerçek Publishing, 1983, p. 67

"Vatan cüda değilim, fakat firakıyla –
  Not away from patrie, yet homesick
muhacirâne gezer ağlarım öz diyarımda"
  Wondering in tears in my own abode"
Mehmed Âkif Ersoy
  Mehmed Âkif Ersoy

"Öz garip, öz vatanında parya"
  "A stranger, a pariah in his fatherland"
Necip Fazıl Kısakürek
  Necip Fazıl Kısakürek

Did the barefoot Anatolian peasant want his son not to be a pariah in his homeland? Psychological factors indeed contribute to this deep concern.

Another approach: Vote for ideology, or services democracy? Sentiment or logic in voting?

Why do people "live in the sewer" voting sentimentally, not for those who would take them to a civilised environment, but for those politicians who keep them in the sewer? Illogical, non-western behaviour. And AKP, champion of services approach, going by Western logic. The modern party of services, of modern infrastructure. Whereas CHP of Ottoman devshirme DNA is against swift change, going against the investment in vital infrastructure with the famous Ottoman rejectionism "istemezük-we reject." And interestingly, living in their illogical sewer environment, they consider themselves civilised, and insist that everyone else live like them. Is this response a resentment-driven reflex of millennia?

The argument that we began the Republic as a classless society can be taken as a basis since there are no aristocrats in our nation, and non-Muslim members of the "Constantinople" bourgeoisie have left.

In his letter of 1923 to Inonu, Atatürk explains the starting point as follows:

"My dear Pasha, I consider you to be the Republic's first prime minister. Hold, and don't reject! You now realise why I picked you. Another major war is coming. As the Front Commander and Chief Turkish Delegate in Lausanne, you are aware of some aspects of our situation, of course.

You informed us after your return from Lausanne that the major powers believed that, given our predicament, we would soon give up. I'll give you a quick rundown of the overall situation, which is even more pitiful than you already realise.

A sickly, indebted country has been passed down to us. We are a destitute, rural nation.

We hardly have any year-round accessible highways. About 4000 km of railroads exist. But we don't even own a meter of it. Our maritime sector is in terrible shape... Everywhere usurers abuse our people... Even though we are ostensibly an agricultural nation, we import the majority of our bread flour. Our livestock is dying from rinderpest. Only 337 doctors, 434 health officers, and 136 midwives are employed in the country. Pharmacies are rare in urban areas. Our people are dying from pandemics. We have three million trachoma patients.

Louse is a serious problem. Our population is sick to the core. Infant deaths exceed 60%. Of the population, 80% live in rural areas. It is mostly nomadic. No phone, no engine, no machine. We import industrial products from abroad. We even import tiles.

Only a small portion of Istanbul and Izmir's districts have access to electricity. 830 villages have been burned by the enemy. There have been 114,408 building fires. Nearly all of the country needs to be rebuilt. More than 400 000 immigrants will come from Greece. Both our economic situation and educational system are in terrible condition.

We have few economists here. Only one-fourth of the children who are of school age can be enrolled. Problem of public education could never have been dealt wih. We must develop the Republic's human capital and fortify the front of our honour.

I wanted to share with you the importance and honour of this monumental undertaking. God help us![49]

According to historian İlber Ortaylı, the table is as follows:

---

[49] Turgut Özakman, Cumhuriyet: Türk Mucizesi 2, Bilgi Publishing, 2010

"In 1920, around 12 million people lived in the country, 11 million residing in villages. No tractors. Hittite practice of primitive plow and oxen were the agricultural way. There were about two million people with malaria, 1 million with syphilis and 3 million with trachoma in Anatolia; Tuberculosis, typhus, and typhoid epidemics were rampant; one out of every two babies born, died before reaching the age of 1; The average life expectancy was about 40 years. Three hundred and thirty-seven doctors, one hundred and sixty pharmacists, and one hundred and six midwives were in the nation. There was no dentist with a license.

The literacy rate was 5% for men and 5% for women.

Literate men were mostly either military officers or non-Muslims. In any case, three out of every four kids of school age did not attend school. Only 23 high schools existed. A third of the teachers lacked even basic preparation for teaching. There was only one university that was superior to the madrasah, Darülfünun. Do you have any idea how many books have been published in the 150 years since Ibrahim Müteferrika (1727)? There were only 417."[50]

With his study, "Türkiye'de Yeni Hayat-New Life in Türkiye", Zafer Toprak perfectly captures the dreadful times we have lived in. Citing Doctor Hakkı Şinasi Pasha: *"Nation's child mortality rate was extremely high— around 80%. The circumstances for the remaining 20% were also dire."*

---

[50] Turgut Özakman, 2010, p. 188

Yes, 80% to 90% of infant deaths occurred before reaching age one. How did the remaining 10% fare?

To this, Sabiha Zekeriya added:

"Orphans were the first to appear. There were about 200,000 of them. The state patronised a small portion of it. 190,000 were left on the streets. Nine out of ten of the kids could not get enough to eat.. Illegitimate children were the third group to experience victimisation. A significant portion of them died on the streets, while others died inside the Darülaceze orphanage. Children being forced to beg on the streets by some "trade companies" was another child tragedy. A sizable portion of the underprivileged children spent the day wandering around and sleeping in mosque courtyards, under bridges, and at the base of fountains. Some of the kids had physical and intellectual disabilities. Among them were the deaf, dumb, blind, and lame. Of the remaining 5% of uneducated children, Sabiha Zekeriya removed lazy, stupid, sluggish, or who were unable to finish their physical development by working in physically demanding jobs, only 2% were left for the future of the nation. How a "modern nation," a "democracy," could be established using this ratio? The Republic's main issue was this."[51]

Why these gloomy facts? I assert. They are the roots of the inferiority complex of our lumpen high society!

They try to forget this gloomy heritage – hating where they came from. They make an effort to put the

---

[51] Turgut Özakman, 2010, p. 189

past behind them, trying to forget the gendarme beatings, the trachoma-ridden peasant grandmothers and grandfathers, and pretending to be of aristocratic heritage. In extreme denial, they think they are Americans. They desire to assimilate into a Christian Western community as soon as possible. It is because of the historical alienating educational philosophy which we still haven't managed to correct. In the Republican era, the ability of Enderun's education to separate the peasant from his original way of life still continued unabated. Today, 90% of young, alienated graduates want to leave the country.

Futhermore, it will not be easy to resolve the atmosphere of hatred in our politics without delving into the psychological depths of these aspiring metropolitan lumpens with diplomas pouring into the streets with "contemporary" and "progressive" claims unaware of the manipulations of foreign interests.

Individual psychological and socio-psychological studies of the lumpen society in Istanbul can shed important light on the serious social disease of alienation from our heritage which plagues our day. We may surmise that, as the process of transformation from peasant to lumpenism to bourgeois, and from social adolescence to maturation, develops in its natural course, hostility to the village and the hatred of the past may gradually decrease.

Another interesting socio-psychological observation: Highly educated, prosperous AKP yuppies, even studied at Ivy League and other best universities of the world, sometimes see those primary school graduate CHP members as a superior class, or "White Tribe", like in the Indian caste system. Deep analysis of this inferior "Black Tribe" psychology, accepting the "Social Stigma" posed on them, needs attention.

Forget those uneducated CHP flock. Those with diplomas, accepted intellectuals of our country, are simply parroting ideas produced in the West without adding anything to them, just memorising the oral cultural genes of Anatolian peasants.

Inspired by Prof. Erol Göka, let's briefly discuss the concepts of white versus black.

An extreme case: The family offers five daily prayers. Father dressed in traditional, rural baggy shalwar, skullcap, and clogs. The child is well-educated, holds a high rank in the public or private sector, has severed ties to his religion, indulges in alcohol and pork consumption, and, if feminine, dons a bikini. She is scared of being seen with her mother wearing a hijab in modern settings. Given her position and feeling cut off from the lifestyle of her family, she also views them with disgust and hatred. Can we now classify this family (Black Turks) and their offspring (White Turks) as belonging to the same social group? How many societies have a significant, radical shift in class within a single generation within the same family?

Our academics have so much work to do on multidisciplinary research on cultural rupture, alienation, and beyond that, self-hatred beginning in the family.

Conservatives

As the saying goes, every political power creates its own bourgeoisie. The faithful Anatolian capital undoubtedly prospered during the AKP era. And quickly, happily started enjoying capitalist consumption. Pious businessmen started to purchase homes in the wealthy areas of the metropols, as well as shop and eat in upscale establishments.

Not to lose focus, our topic is still not Anatolia's underprivileged. We're talking about a new capitalist class emerging from Anatolia to challenge the old capitalists and the old Westernised bureaucracy. A new class rising to modernity, yet refusing to be alienated, trying to cling to its traditional culture.

If an aristocracy does arise in the twenty-first century, it will, in my opinion, do so from conservative religious capital rather than the volatile, liberal, cosmopolitan capital. The aristocratic class holds (as far as it can keep) traditional values. It rejects eradicating roots, frequent changes, and sharp class changes. Therefore, the likelihood that the Turkish aristocracy of the future will be made up of pious capital is higher than that of liberalist, globalist capitalists.

As for culture, one of the main reasons why Westernernists have disdain for the new religious bourgeoisie is its modern cultural defects. And the pious new bourgeois is meek to meet the accusation. In actuality, by making this accusation, Westerner white

Turks are shooting themselves in the heel because they are sleeping in the conformity of parroting what is produced in the West. Since 19th Century Tanzimat, they are just the compradors, "consumers", and "distributors" of culture and concepts developed in the West.

Here are Toynbee's words once more: *"We are right to denigrate Türkiye. Why should we respect those who copy us? I only respect people who add to my civilisation."*

In their sleep and conformity, and self-praise, they have no rooted incentive to create a challenging culture against the West. Except for a few, they do not have enough authentic "Turkish" production to be presented to the world. Not in literature, except for a few, in music, architecture, technology, or the visual arts. Because their "closed peasant ideology Kemalism" of the 1940s neither has universal ethical, nor aesthetic concerns. It seems illogical to expect genuine cultural innovation from people who have been comfortably sleeping on Western culture for nearly two centuries. Expecting local, authentic cultural Turkish values to rise from the alienated, unrooted Western clones was a grave mistake.

With President Erdoğan, the new Anatolian bourgeois started to feel the pain, and this new bourgeois was the candidate to give birth to genuine Turkish modernity. For the awakening, Erdoğan does not hesitate to cooperate with the old İstanbul capital and get their support in opening new joint museums and culture centers too.

Ending this section, a comic narrative of the 1968 youth: A walking library hailing from the village tradition of his grandfathers and oral culture of memorising the Qur'an, now a Marxist, tests the memorisation of another peasant-origin Marxist friend. He commands his mate to recite a certain sentence from a certain page of Das Kapital. Parroting was all they needed. No philosophising.

Or take a Kemalist eager to gain respectability in the traditional verbal memorisation culture, reciting Atatürk aphorisms in his modern group. And the sterility and lack of philosophical and intellectual creativity for modern Turkish society, and further, for the rest of the world.

Taking a break, in the footsteps of his 19th Century Young Turc brothers' "Mission Civilisatrice" tradition, shepherding the flock, let's hear our student from American Robert College in İstanbul again:

The year is 1951. "Robert College taught us about American ideals. Now I try to pass these on to our peasants who are poor, ignorant and opposed to change. In the face of these hurdles, our best weapon is the Americans, good books and good ways."[52]

About twenty years later, this time, the youth of 1968. Shepherds are coming from the left. Take the neighbouring schools Ankara University Faculty of

---

[52] Babaoğlu, Sabah Newspaper, ibid, Hiperlink: https://bit.ly/3RkTX8E

Political Sciences Mülkiye (where I was a lecturer) and Faculty of Law, my school. The time when the parka-combat-boot-moustache was in fashion. The so-called leftist Cumhuriyet newspaper was placed in the parka's pocket with care. Young peasant students claimed to change the order. They said they were socialists. However, their subconscious, which they were unaware of, operated differently.[53] They were the same peasants who came to college to be alienated from their peasant families, and then joined the ruling elite cadres. To lead the backward peasant society was the motivation behind leaving the village and joining the devshirme class. Proof? Many of those 1968ers are the high society of İstanbul championing Americanism and capitalism in their grey 70s.

---

[53] Listen to what Dris Kucukomer has to say: "The leftists in Turkey are reactionary. The growth of the productive forces is opposed by them. They support an authoritarian, top-down, single-centered system of government. They view the populace as a herd that needs to be led."

PART TWO

Ottoman Empire

In the first section, we made an effort to look as closely as we could at the psychological underpinnings of the current climate of political hatred, including the inferiority complex, the fear of rejection, aspirants, conformism, and the political hatred they incite. Let's now attempt to shed light on the origins of this hatred. The Ottoman ruler (devshirme) and the ruled (reâyâ) are our subjects. These two groups are alienated from each other.

This section will begin with an excerpt from "The Day Lasts More Than a Hundred Years and The White Cloud of Genghis Khan," a famous book[54] by renowned Kyrgyz author Cengiz Aytmatov. Our story is based on an ethnic Kazakh Soviet bureaucrat, who left his village and became alienated from his village during the Union of Soviet Socialist Republics (USSR), based on the example of mankurt:[55]

---

[54] Under the title "The White Cloud of Genghis Khan," Aitmatov later published the portion of his book that he was unable to complete because of the Soviet government. The TV shows Diriliş Erturul and Payitaht Abdulhamid also featured the mankurt theme, as viewers will recall.

[55] The one who is alienated from the national identity, alienated from the society they live in.

"This legend dates back to the time when the Juan-Juans were driven from the borders of Southeast Asia and raided North to capture Yellow-Ozek.

He knew nothing; he was like a newborn. His name, as well as the names of his mother and father, were unknown to him. He also had no recollection of the harm the Juan-Juans had inflicted upon him. Every question he was asked was met with a yes, a no, or silence. He never removed the hat, which was firmly fastened to his head. It was unfortunate and extremely painful, but sometimes people enjoyed making fun of the disabled. The camel skin that some mankurts were wearing caused the traders to start laughing and making fun of it. There would be nothing more frightening than such a mankurt saying, "Come, let's steam your head and tear off that camel's skin." Hearing this word, the mankurt would kick like a wild bear and would not let anyone touch his head.

They never took off their hats, they slept with them day and night. According to guest merchants, although they were clumsy, they were doing their jobs very well.

- Your name is Colaman. Do you hear? You are Colaman. Your father's name was Dönenbay. Don't you remember your father too? He taught you to shoot arrows when you were little. I am your mother and you are my son. You are from the tribe of the Naymans. Do you understand? You are a Nayman...

...

All these words reminded Mankurt of nothing, and did not affect him. But Mother Nayman continued to speak, hoping to awaken something in her son's dark subconscious. She was talking over and over, asking the same questions persistently, as if slamming a tightly closed door:

- Colaman! My son!

Nayman Ana suddenly spun in the saddle and saw her son aiming at her.

- Stop! Don't throw!

She just had time to say it. And wanted to spur the camel to speed it up, but the thrown arrow whizzed and stabbed into her left flank!

The blow was deadly. Mother Nayman's head drooped, she wanted to hug the camel's neck, but she could not hold on and fell to the ground. But before her, her white muslin headscarf fell from her head. And the muslin became a bird and took off. It flew into the sky, repeating the last words that came out of the mother's mouth: "Remember your name! Remember who you are! Your father's name is Dönenbay! Dönenbay! Dönenbay!"

Trains run from east to west and from west to east in these locations…

Let's take this Sabitcan as an illustration. From a young age, they sent him to a boarding school. Then they placed him in various colleges and universities. Poor Kazangap had sacrificed everything to ensure that his only son would receive a quality education and lead a happy life. What came out of it? Despite the many lessons learned, he was still useless and worthless

....

Your father raised and educated you. And now, we leave him in peace in the middle of the desolate steppe, alone in his grave. The fact that this is our own country and home is the only solace we have. You are a well-educated man who has a responsibility in the city. Thank God you have a way with words, you get along with everyone, and you read all kinds of books.

- What if I read it? Sabitcan interrupted.

... Old Yedigey was thinking about these, and the more he thought about it, the more he felt crushed, and he was writhing in unbearable heartache. He was both angry and pitying this young man called Sabitcan and murmured in hatred of him:

- You are a mankurt, you are a mankurt! A real mankurt!"

Leaving the village, becoming estranged from his roots and not recognizing one's mother and ancestors...

Three Ottomans
Classes in the Ottoman Empire

Like a novice approaching Islamic sciences unprepared, his faith is shaken; a Turk entering Ottoman history without sufficient background knowledge might come to dislike his Ottoman ancestors too. Proceeding from the psychological background, now enter the contentious relationship of the modern Turk and his Ottoman ancestor.

This book is penned with the knowledge that Ottomans and today's Turks are one essence, like a father and son who could not get along, that they together were the founders of one of the greatest civilizations in human history, in comparative history, at a time when serfs in feudal Europe were suffering in dark ages. This book does not try to defame the Turk, but to analyse the roots of its internal political schism.

Let's listen to Jean-Paul Roux: *"The eternal state is the production of the nomadic spirit. There is a general consensus among historians about the high state-building skills of the Turks. Turks have a tendency to establish an empire. Turks are literally the rulers of the earth. The empires they founded, and none alike, have had some basic features for two millennia. These empires were mosaics of people: Turks tried to keep peoples together in harmony, giving them the right to preserve their identities, languages, cultures, religions, and often even their leaders, under the rule of a strongly centralized and despotic power. Although they held the highest duties as the right of conquest, if the people of the country they conquered were civilized, they did not hesitate to bring the local people to positions that required trust.*"[56]

Prof. Ahmet Taşağıl agrees: *"To say that only Turks resided within the borders of Türkiye would not be right. There were also residents of other nationalities, some of whom attained the position of vizier. This rise occasionally had negative effects. Because they could be effective on the emperor and change the laws. This could try the limits of bringing the state to collapse. There was a schism between the people and the government."*[57]

In short, we do not doubt our nobility as one of the greatest nations in history. Returning to our subject, there is a history riddle that needs to be questioned before us. The Republican ideology did not qualify its historical arch enemy the West as the "other". Instead, the "religious-regressive-bigot" Ottoman Empire was the "other". "The bigoted Ottoman" is guilty, he is the "other". However, there is a surprise. Starting with Conqueror Fatih, while the sultans tried not to share power with the Turkish aristocracy, they left their fate to the mercy of the janissaries and devshirme bureaucracy.

---

[56] Jean Paul Roux, Türklerin Tarihi, Pasifik'ten Akdeniz'e 2000, Trans. Aykut Kazancıgil and Lale Arslan-Özcan, Kabalcı Publishing, Istanbul, 2007, p. 41

[57] Türklerin Serüveni - Metehan'dan Attila'ya, Fatih'ten Atatürk'e, Ed. Cansu Canan Ülgen, Kronik Book, Istanbul, 2019, p. 30

Then comes the question:

Ottoman is guilty, let us admit, but which Ottoman?

We're confused. Let's approach the subject analytically. There are three Ottomans. All three of them are our ancestors: The Sultan, Devshirme Bureaucracy, and Reâyâ (rural people). So are we the enemies of our very selves?

Let's take a closer look at our topic. Start with Plato, the striking subject: The distinction between the ruler and the ruled. Later, while reading Arnold Toynbee, we see his description of the Ottoman Devshirme Institution as the closest system to Plato's ideal governance system. First of all, my late friend and elder Halil Inalcik, then Şerif Mardin, plus many historians and sociologists mention the centre-periphery institutions as 'seyfiye-military', 'ilmiye-academia', courthouse, bureaucracy, reâyâ and so on.

We may say every society has its elite who are more culturally advanced than those who live in rural areas. What did this alienation mean for the Ottoman Empire? What social and political effects? What are the subsequent effects still being felt in Türkiye in the 21st century?

Europe did have traditional classes of its feudal, then capitalist system. Was there no class in the Ottoman Empire? There were definitely two classes in tension. Plato's ruling versus ruled classes. The second subject of our book is the thousand-year-old devshirme management system, which started with the Seljuks and continued in the Ottoman Empire, and ended with the July 15, 2016 Revolution.[58]

The Sultan

Now let's examine the suspects one by one. Let's start with the sultan.

Founding Father, Osman Bey, a Turk, his successors except for a few, were born of non-Turkish slave concubines. Turkmen were dominant in the era of rise. With the establishment of the Janissaries and the devshirme bureaucracy during Murad I's reign, and institutionalised in the time of Fatih, the power is now with the devshirme bureaucracy. Concubines, the mothers of sultans, grand viziers and princes, were raised in the same elite colleges Enderun and Harem. In other words, the sultan himself was educated in the devshirme school too. There are no relatives. No family. Fraternal murder is legalized. In this system, there is no aristocracy to rival the power. The government is in the hands of the devshirme bureaucracy. The system overthrows and kills the sultan it does not want.[59] There is no Europe-like "Feudal Aristocracy" or "Vatican" as balancing forces.[60]

---

[58] Arnold Toynbee, A Study of History, Vol. 3, The Growth of Civilizations, p. 33
[59] Kucukomer, ibid. p. 19
[60] "Although the absolute will of the Sultan/Caliph seems to represent the central authority, the courtiers, the army, the bureaucracy and the ulema are also influential in decisions and practices; The balance between them deteriorated over time.

Back to the beginning. The sultan is on the back of the tiger (devshirme). You are either the master or the victim.[61] If you are strong, you rule. If you don't, you fall. Such was the Platonist devshirme state administration. The real owner of the state in Arnold Toynbee's description, was the devshirme bureaucrats who overthrew twelve sultans and the very same bureaucrats who founded the Republic when the state collapsed.

In such an intertwined, homogeneous administration, can it be said that only the sultan is guilty? Or, we can opt for the next suspect. Was it the devshirme bureaucracy responsible for the collapse of a grand empire? The Ottoman devshirme generals who founded the Republic made this mistake. They said that the culprit was the sultan. They did this on purpose. They attributed

---

The Kapıkulu Hearths, which hold the armed power when the balance is disturbed, gain a more effective position against the others". Goka, 2006, ibid. p. 231

[61] Kagan was "the representative of the Sky-God on earth." Zeki Velidi Togan, Introduction to General Turkish History, Enderun Bookstore, Istanbul, 1970, p.185.

"In addition to nature cults, another primordial faith intertwined with the nomadic mood is the cult of ancestors. The ancient Turks believed that the spirits of the ancestors also continued to live, that they were a part of their own lives, they gave great importance to the spirits of the ancestors and made sacrifices dedicated to them. It is very easy to understand why the nomadic Turks, who constantly live together in solidarity and discipline, develop a tight bond with their relatives, and why they show such respect for the spirits of their dead ancestors, whom they had to entrust to nature. The cult of ancestors is probably closely related to the nomadic solidarity and the need for strict discipline..." Erol Göka, 2012, ibid. p. 155

all the responsibilities of the Ottoman collapse process to the "sultan". They could not do otherwise. The demonization of Abdulhamid and Vahdettin was a practical, Machiavellian political approach.

The early Republican rulers could not stone themselves, as they were the uninterrupted continuation of the Ottoman devshirme bureaucrats (Young Turk-İttihat Terakki). The devshirme bureaucracy class should not have been responsible for the collapse of the Ottoman Empire; a devil had to be found responsible, and the devil was the sultan. That is, it was an individual, not the system.

Let's take a breath and think here. In the Ottoman administrative mechanism, the Sultan and Devshirme were one body. As we said at the beginning, when Atatürk got rid of the sultan, he cut off the head of the devshirme. The interesting thing is that the devshirme did not feel the pain at first, and did not realize that being headless would soon bring about its own demise. Although the beheaded devshirme continued its rule for roughly a hundred more years with its historical experience, it eventually gave up and lost its millennial power.

In summary, loading all blame for the Ottoman collapse on one person, the sultan, was a political tactic freeing the devshirme ruling class from responsibility. Ottoman generals and founders of the Republic could not do better.

Although the period of Ottoman decline and collapse is seen as a natural process from the point of view of Ibn Khaldoun, what makes sense is that the responsibility of a historical process lies with the system, not individuals. Hence, the Ottoman Empire was not just the sultan.

Now let's look at the Devshirme administration.

Devshirme Bureaucracy

"Whoever became a learned person of the Turks, have been alienated to their nation, people."[62]

- Ömer Seyfettin

For Prof. İdris Küçükömer, the Ottoman Empire was a military-state in constant semi-mobilization.

Actually, what made the Ottoman Empire one of the longest Empires of European history was its devshirme bureaucracy system and Fatih's law of fratricide. Comparing Roman and Ottoman Imperial maps, one can vividly see the remarkable similarity between them, the Ottoman map being the shrunken form of Roman territories, and that the Ottoman Empire was the continuation of the Roman Empire. Devshirme system, in a way, continues in the USA, together with Ivy League colleges doing what Enderun College did for the Ottoman elite, ruling heteregenous ethnicities and religious sects. An interesting field for academic research?

---

[62] Ömer Seyfeddin, Halk ne der?, [Article], Türk Sözü

The main problem that draws our attention starting from Central Asia is as Turkic states settled and transformed from nomad to sedentary status, the state saw the nomadic democracy (toy-kurultay) and the settled feudal Turkish aristocracy as a threat to its political power.

"Lords of the Horizons"[63], conquerors with their swords, yet lacking settled administration experience, Turkish Khans felt the need to recruit civil servants from the educated people of the countries they conquered.[64] The problem was that, a ruling class (Ak Budun), which is increasingly alienated from the Turkmen, was turning into a power centre by separation from the founding core (Kara Budun). Seljuks and the Ottomans were the two great states where the alienation of the administration from the "Turkmen" peaked.

The process began in the 14th century with Sultan Murad I's need for regular soldiers. There is a 'pencik'

---

[63] Jason Goodwin's name for his book. Full title of the book: Lords of the Horizons: A History of the Ottoman Empire
[64] "The Turks were experiencing the dilemma of having to realize their endless ideal of administrating with borrowed cultures and devshirmes. Moreover, the Turkish aristocracy, the white elite, who adored borrowed cultures, was becoming more and more alienated than ever to consider itself as the same root as the black underdog. Of course, retaining the privilege of using force would have caused any state some alienation from its subjects, but the alienation of the Turkish power was not like that. On the one hand, he was breaking from his kin, and on the other, establishing his army from them. The nation had to become an 'army-nation'. Goka, 2006, ibid. p. 196

rule in the Islamic tradition. One-fifth of the war booty slaves belonged to the sultan. Until then, the sultan did not use his 1/5 share of slaves except for minor private needs. Çandarlı Halil Pasha proposes to enlist the slaves of the sultan's share in the army. Thus, with the order of Sultan Murat I, the foundation of the janissary was laid in 1361. Later, children from the Balkans were gathered and recruited for this purpose. Given to Turkish families and Turkified, they were sent to janissary barracks. And the smart ones were sent to the palace college, Enderun, to be bureaucrats, to be the future generals and grand viziers of the Empire. Such was the governing devshirme system.

As for the slave girls, they were sent to harem, the girls' college, and employed in palace services. Smart ones could rise to be the concubines and a few became the sultan's favourite and, finally the mother of the next emperor, the *valide sultan* (queen mother). Harem also gave its girls to devshirme bureaucrats and generals who were also the slaves of the state, without roots.

However, let us repeat: what is meant by the word "devshirme" is not a non-Muslim slave official in the narrow sense. That part is the period of approximately one hundred and fifty years between Fatih and Murad III. What is broadly meant by the five-hundred-year-old devshirme, is the statesman who was taken from his village, trained in the palace college, and "alienated" to his origin. Viewed from this projection, the alienation of today's educated elite from their rural parents, to the values of their families, is the continuation of such a historical education process.[65]

And alienation was much deeper in the cultural sphere. Sociologist Ziya Gokalp, who deeply influenced Atatürk's ideas, strongly expresses this distinction in his "Principles of Turkism". Ottoman history, as defined by Şerif Mardin, is, in a sense, the history of the tension between the central devshirme bureaucracy and the peripheral Turkmen people.

An anecdote of the late 19th century. One day, Sultan Abdulhamid II looks at his garden from his palace window. A gardener mistakenly splashes mud at a passerby Albanian-origin Ottoman officer. "Donkey Turk! Be careful,"[66] the officer says. The sultan interferes from the window. "I am a Turk too!" The sultan's recollection of being Turkish is a belated realisation of his roots in the course of history, an acceptance that doesn't make much sense at the autumn of a dying empire.

Here, another anecdote may be explanatory. Between 1980 and 1982, I was managing the Consular Branch of the Turkish Embassy in Jeddah, Saudi Arabia. One day, I received an invitation from the prison commander to talk about a Turkish detainee. When I

---

[65] "The fact that devshirme hide their Christianity in themselves and appear to be Islamized... Their adoption of Bektashism was a typical example of the 'double morality' approach, which is the most basic indicator of the mafiosi society." Goka, 2006, ibid. p. 231

[66] Mustafa Armağan, One Atsız, two Abdülhamids (1), Yeni Akit Newspaper, 30 October 2022, Hyperlink: https://bit.ly/3DzDgjU

went, a private greeted me, and took me to his lieutenant colonel. While we were waiting for the detainee, we started a friendly and humorous conversation with the commander. After a while, the private joined the conversation. There came a moment in the cheerful atmosphere, when the private slapped the lieutenant colonel on the shoulder and shouted: "Ya ammiy-Uncle!" I didn't show any reaction at the moment. But did a lot of contemplation later.

I thought about how the devshirme culture divides like a knife: the ruler and the ruled, the official behind the desk and the citizen, the commander and the soldier. I found the opportunity to compare strict Turkish discipline and hierarchy with that of the egalitarian, democratic tribal tradition. In the Bedouin culture of equality, rank did not mean much for the private and his commander.

The alienation of the Ottoman devshirme bureaucracy from the Anatolian Turkmen became more acute with Westernization in the 19th century. The word "Etrak-ı bi-idrak – mindless Turks" of the devshirme continued in the bureaucratic vocabulary of the early Republic with the words of the governor of Ankara, "You, Anatolian ox!"[67]. General İsmet İnönü, addressing his officers at the war theater warned them: "The people are

---

[67] "When the Turkish race were interested in, and wanted to learn the crafts required by the settled life, this was not welcomed by the capital and the rulers. Because the Turkish race were needed as soldiers, shepherds and farmers". (Babaoğlu, 2008: p.129) Göka, 2012, ibid, p. 187

your enemy"[68]. And finally, 21st century elite mockery for the underdog "belly scratchers". Historical schism continues unabated.

Yet this is the very elite which floated the state ship in stormy oceans with the experience of centuries. A system which prolonged the life of a corrupt empire. They were the real owners of the state. As the Ottoman Empire sank, this very bureaucracy founded a new, dynamic Republic from its ashes. The founders of the Republic were the very bureaucrats and generals educated in Sultan Abdülhamid II's schools.

And 21st century. People's Revolution of 15 July 2016. People topple devshirmes. Seize the state from the historical rulers. Push generals to their barracks. Now the elite pushed away from a state it had founded, disheartened, further seeing it at the hands of the new rural stock, turns bitter, and hostile against the very state it built. Together with devshirmes, their lumpen aspirants, who have not yet internalized modern democracy and modern humanitarian values, also become enemies of the people's revolution.

The process is seen in the West as a religious warfare, Islamists versus Secularists. It is distortion par excellence, if not ignorance. This is the continuation of a historical schism between the Turkmen who lost their state to the

---

[68] "Just as the Great Seljuks started taking names such as Sancar and Tuğrul in an effort to return to their relatives and ancestors near their collapse, the Ottomans also remembered their Turkish roots". (Cahen, 1994: p.54), Kucukömer, ibid. p. 76

alienated devshirme and are now grasping it back. It is a class warfare in Marxist, Platonist outlook. Indeed, religion and tradition versus modernity and positivism are characteristics of the two classes. Yet it is not Islamists versus secularists as Westerners want to see it. This is a "class war" in the technical sense.

Let's repeat Idris Kucukomer about religious/secular rhetoric:

"In Türkiye, the Orientalist-Islamist movement is one of the two main currents that have aimed to steer and save the Ottoman society in the last hundred years. The other is the westernmost-secular movement. This last trend, in historical development, is the permanent antithesis of the Islamist current. The important aspect of the westernist current is that it appears as a current that prevents the emergence of a real thesis."[69]

Despite the philosophy of coexistence with the "other," which has been present in the culture of Islam and nomadic Turks from the very beginning, the practice of either destroying or assimilating the "other" by the Western civilization and its local clones must have inspired Küçükömer to pen these lines.

Reâyâ (Periphery)

Now let us see if we can stone the reaya, the Turkmen as the devil. Can Turkmen be held responsible for the collapse of the Ottoman Empire? In the founding years of the Republic, yes, the Turkmen were also blamed for

---

[69] Kucukomer, ibid. p. 13

the collapse. The Ottoman devshirme bureaucrats, the founders of the Republic, blamed not only the sultan but also the reaya, whom they had excluded and despised for centuries. They accused the Turkish peasant as a backward religious bigot responsible for the collapse.

What was the reality? Iran's Turkmen rulers had converted Persians into Shia. Knowing the tension in the Ottoman system between the founding Turkmen and its devshirme rulers, they also tried to manipulate their kin, Shia Turkmens, against the Ottoman regime. And with a strong example, Turkmen had betrayed Sultan Bayezid for his dependence on his Serbian soldiers rather than his own Turkmen kin, and sided with Tamerlane in the Ankara war of 1402. Hence, the devshirme system forced Turkmen nomads to settle and convert to the Sunni sect.

Come 21st Century Republic. Secularism is the code of the day. This time, force the Turkmen out of orthodox Sunni practice into a protestantized secular version of Islam where religion is pushed out of social life, locking it into individual hearts.

The package of blame also included Alevi Turkmen fathers, pilgrim elders, hodjas, sect leaders, Kurdish religious scholars and the widespread village masses who were subject to them. The periphery was regressive, reactionary. It had to be secularized. The literature of the period was brutally oppressing the religious culture of the peasants. This was a great injustice. In fact, the nomadic, rural Turkish understanding of Islam, with its Bektashism and mysticism, was the most tolerant, softest, and even liberal Islam of the Islamic world throughout history.[70]

At this point, let's hear Erol Goka. *"Writing is the antidote to oral culture, which is the fertile environment of all kinds of reaction and status quo because it is based on memorization, remembering and repetition."*[71] Yes, the village is verbal, yes, the village is conservative. But when we put it on the scale, the janissaries and the artisans of Istanbul were indeed more closed to innovations.

Yet in the eyes of the devshirmes, it was everyone else but themselves that was responsible for backwardness and collapse. The treacherous sultan and bigoted Anatolia were responsible for the decline and fall of the Ottoman Empire. Literature dealt with these issues.

For the founders of the Republic, Europe was not the historical "other". The "other" was the Ottoman. Its sultan and his Turkmen reaya. Even in our day, it is such a psychological quagmire as when some devshirme is reading the İzmir March or Republican Tenth Year Anniversary March, the "other" in their minds is not the Greek who attempted to invade Anatolia, but the Turk, the continuation of the Ottoman nomad.

---

[70] Sabri F. Ülgener, Zihniyet ve Din İslam, Tasavvuf ve Çözülme Devri İktisat Ahlâkı, Der Publishing, Istanbul, 2006, p. 67
[71] Erol Göka, 2006, ibid. p. 224

Let's remember the lines of Erol Goka. *"So much so that the Chinese are stunned by the internal quarrels of the Turks, and the Turks would rather destroy each other than live side by side in peace. They are hostile to each other... They say they consist of tens of thousands of clans."* Add General Inonu's words to his officers in the middle of the war: *"The people are your enemy".*

Abandonment of the Turks who remained in the Arab countries to assimilation, and the Turks who were massacred in the Balkans to their fate, is the manifestation of the government's indifference and disconnectedness from the people. In the same line, the murder of Turkish diplomats by Armenian terrorists in the 1980s was also a "state issue" requiring the attention of the state bureaucracy, not the public. The people did not yet realize that the damage to the government would directly affect their personal and class interests. Apart from military service and taxes, Turks had neither much relationship with the state nor any expectation from the state.

Let's go back to our first question: Who is the Ottoman?

We all are! Ottoman with its sultan, devshirme and Turkmen are all our fathers. We are their descendants, period.[72]

---

[72] "Ottoman, of course, was Turkish. What are they discussing? If not, why did foreigners call the XV and XVI centuries 'Turkish Century'? There is nothing to discuss because it is the sequel of the Göktürks. It is so as a state tradition, and even more so as a people". Ahmet Taşağıl, The

There was hatred between them, there was tension, there were riots, and there were murders, yes. But the fight was between our grandfathers. Just as we see its absolute projection in today's politics... Nobody can choose their mother, father or ancestor. Like other nations, we are descendants of those who fell into our destiny. Our concern is how the Republic can repair the alienation of devshirme-reaya, which is an Ottoman disease. Although we deal with the conflicts among ourselves in this book, we should never forget that.

Arnold Toynbee and many other thinkers regard the Ottoman Empire as one of the greatest civilizations in human history.[73] We built it. And we are justifiably proud of it. Maybe with another book, we will have the opportunity to explain the sublime aspects of our Empire.

Janissary Revolts

Let's go back and take a look at our origins, the devshirme revolts against the sultan.

Adventure of Turks From Metehan to Attila, From Fatih to Atatürk, Ed. Cansu Canan Ülgen, Chronic Book, Istanbul, 2019, p. 36

[73] As you know, in Medieval Europe there was a feudal aristocracy to balance the kings. There was also the source of legitimacy, the Pope. (Pope Gregory VI had the King of France, Henry IV, wait at his door barefoot in the winter of 1077 and begged for forgiveness.) In Erol Göka's words, the Turk is a nomad who "mediates between civilizations, destroys frozen civilizations and prepares an opportunity for a new one to replace them". But in the end he succeeded in establishing his own civilization.

Already mentioned, the origin of the devshirme goes back to the Janissaries, which started in the reign of Murad I and became institutionalized in the reign of Murad II. And a few years after its establishment, its first rebellion was the Buçuktepe Rebellion against the child sultan Mehmed II (Fatih). It is worth mentioning that these janissaries also plundered Istanbul as soon as they received the news of Fatih's death. In the words of Ahmet Önal and Erhan Afyoncu, *"There is hardly an Ottoman sultan who did not face rebellion after Fatih Sultan Mehmed"*.

The characteristic of the janissary is that, it was the first regular European army of its era. There is no other regular force to balance it, neither at home nor in Europe. The devshirme system was a military-civil bureaucrat rule. Although the sultan's power seemed absolute when he was powerful, the administration was still in the hands of the devshirme. For this reason, no one thought of changing the dynasty, except for a few thoughts during coups.

There was learned helplessness in the sultans who destroyed the Anatolian feudalism and rearguard aristocracy and handed over their fate to the Janissaries. Perhaps this unconsciously learned helplessness was effective on the sultans' shortcomings in precaution, negligence and delays in breaking revolts, which we see again and again in the uprisings.

The advice given to the sultans clearly shows this helplessness. *"My Sultan, these mufsids (mischief-makers) need to be calmed down and they cannot be answered in any other way... These servants have taken what they wanted, even from the previous sultans... But God forbid, if these bad habits are not calmed, the situation will be difficult and the state will be in disarray."*[74]

Likewise, Niccolò Machiavelli also has advice to the Ottoman sultans. *"... the prince must get on well with these soldiers, forget the obedient people. Since the prince is completely in the hands of the soldiers, he must take good care of them."*[75]

In his epistle, Koçi Bey states that the central army was getting too strong and said, *"The great sultans in the past used to control the people of six companies; the janissary corps and its individuals, with the corps of the six companies, and control these two gangs with the zeamet and timar soldiers. Now the timar corps has completely disappeared. Now that the military service is given to the control of the janissaries and the cavalry, each of them became a monster."*[76]

When the balancing role of the Anatolian aristocracy and cavalry disappeared, it could be thought that the sultan would use the Janissaries and the Kapikulu Sipahi as a counterbalance to each other, like today's Saudi

---

[74] Erhan Afyoncu, Ahmet Önal, Uğur Demir, Osmanlı İmparatorluğu'nda Askerî Darbeler
ve İsyanlar, Yeditepe Publishing, Istanbul, 2018, p. 12
[75] Niccolo Machiavelli, Hükümdar, Dergah Publications, Istanbul, 2023 [First edition, 1532 with the name "De Principatibus"], p. 83
[76] Erhan Afyoncu, Ahmet Önal, Uğur Demir, ibid. p. 65

dynasty, which has three separate military powers that balance each other. Janissaries and the Cavalry "Kapikulu Sipahi" used to get into serious conflicts from time to time. However, the Janissaries who suppressed the Kapikulu Sipahi Rebellion of 1648 became unchallenged after that event. Such balancing opportunity, not much appreciated before, has also disappeared.

At this point, palace guards come to mind. When coups and rebellions started, was there an inner shield, that is, an army of guards, to protect the sultan? Yes, there were guards called bostancı. Just like Republican Presidential Regiment Commanders betraying Presidents and getting orders from coup juntas, Ottoman bostancıs also used to betray the sultans.

Another parallel with the coup d'états of the Republic, university professors supporting and encouraging generals for coups, were indeed the successors of the Ottoman ulema, giving fatwa-consent to topple the sultans. In particular, the Shaykh al-Islam fatwas were a solid support in this regard.

Guild Revolts

As we said before, the word to summarize the Ottoman Empire's approach to the societies it ruled is the word "lakayt" (indifferent). The state was extremely liberal in the Turkish-Mongol steppe tradition. Apart from collecting taxes for the centre, it did not care at all about the cultures, religions and lifestyles of the millets it ruled.

Compare it with the impositions of lifestyles by the "modern" states?

Within the millet system of religious communities, each religious group was led by its religious leader in its day-to-day affairs. The only concern of the centre was the welfare of the army and the people of Istanbul. The tax system, called internal exploitation by some writers, served to keep this order healthy. Roughly half of Istanbul's population was military and civilian Muslim, while the other half was non-Muslim. In other words, the imperial taxes worked not for the periphery Turkmen, but for the welfare of the happy few of Istanbul. Or else… there would be a riot.[77]

Istanbul's economy contributed to the originating of revolts of Janissaries, tradesmen and ulema were not ineffective like the undisciplined Celali revolts of the Turkmen in the countryside. The sultan was overthrown.

Revolts of Istanbul's economic failures accelerated with rise and expansion, hence the spoils of war stopped and forced the government to heavy internal taxation. The reduction of gold and silver in money (devaluation) due to economic crises led to inflation. Both the janissaries and the artisans of Istanbul suffered from this. For this reason, the cooperation of these two was seen in many rebellions.

---

[77] Kucukömer, ibid. P. 41, "Enver Ziya Karal says that this unit was created by the janissaries, the ulema and the people of Istanbul". p. 53

Although not an exact analogy, military-business cooperation shows the historical continuity in the support and provocation of the military coup by the capital of Istanbul and the press it controls during the Republican coups in times of economic crises.

One of the reasons for the revolts, especially since the 17th century, was the soldiers who returned from the wars, deserted the army and grouped in the cities, unemployed and unpaid. Interestingly, the revolters first held the imperial treasurer and viziers responsible and demanded their heads. In comparison with the republican juntas, bureaucrats of the Republic did not revolt because of the low salary. Because in a country where there was no industry, the bureaucrats, even if their salaries were low, were always in a better and guaranteed situation compared to the rural people on the border of starvation.

A feature of the revolts was the steppe culture of plundering the khan's house under his consent, though this time with a vengeance. So the encouraging aspect of the coups was the custom of plundering the mansions of the "viziers" including the imperial palace, in each coup. The plunder of the palace by the Ottoman officers who overthrew Sultan Abdulhamid II is still a sad memory.

In the Ottoman culture, neither the people nor the state tolerated capital accumulation. But even though it was known that it would be lost one day, bureaucrats still tried to collect worldly goods as much as possible.

H. Ertürk says of the Unionist coup leaders of 1908, *"They made the beginning of the new era with the looting of Yıldız Palace." It is written that everything from jewellery accumulated over 33 years to carpets, chandeliers, curtains, kitchen sets, furniture, and even carved doors were looted in Yıldız Palace. Poet Tevfik Fikret is famous for depictig this plunder; "Eat, misters, eat, this inn of plunder is yours".*[78]

Celali Revolts

First a lengthy quote:[79]

"(Shiite-Sunni conflict in the known sense will only emerge at the end of the XVth century and the beginning of the XVIth century.) In Ottoman expansion into Anatolia and the Balkans, state was greatly aided by sheikhs, fathers, dervishes, and ahis, also known as Khorasan saints.[80]

Although the Ottoman state was founded with the overflowing religious fervour of Akhism and Bektashis; as the state advanced towards an Empire, it started inclining towards sunniism.

Especially after the conquest of Istanbul and, in particular, after the acceptance of the Caliphate, the

---

[78] "Enver Ziya Karal says that this union was created by the janissaries, the ulama and the people of Istanbul". p.53
[79] Ünver Günay, Harun Güngör, Türklerin Dinî Tarihi, Rağbet Publishing, Istanbul, 2003, p.239-439 Küçükömer, ibid. p. 41,
[80] Göka, 2006, ibid S. 183

ambitious, conciliatory, and tolerant understanding of Islam left its place to the increasing authority of the official madrassah and religious nature of the government.

A centralized, semi-theocratic structure akin to that of Byzantium was assumed, and efforts were made to keep sheikhs, saints, and dervish lodges under control."

To remember, one of the first decisions of Atatürk was to establish the Republican version of Ottoman Şeyhül İslam, the Presidency of Religious Affairs and strictly controlled the sheikhs, saints and the lodges, in the footsteps of Ottoman state tradition. Religion was important to the state. Turkmen could not be left to its archaic religious leaders.

The most important element for the transformation of sociopolitical disturbances into action is the need for an ideology to die for. In the social unrests before the age of ideologies, the values to die for were religions and sects. If we consider the 20th century as the age of ideologies and the post-modern 21st century as the age of the death of ideologies, we may guess that religions and sects may pop up again in Europe as useful tools for social unrest.

In short, today's religious-secularist fight is class warfare in the technical sense between Anatolian Turks and the devshirme bureaucracy, and just like its Ottoman predecessor, the people are suppressed with accusations of reactionism, regressionism and bigotry. The Western world, adamant about seeing secular, Westernized autocrats in developing Muslim countries, also provokes this accusation.

We can trace the origins of our topic back to the Turkmen Babai uprising of 13th century, which arose in response to Seljuks' alteration of their land-rule policy. Though seen as a religious uprising against the injustice of the state, it was not only Alevis but also Kurds, Sunnis, and non-Muslims in the affair, hence suggesting that religion was used as a "tool" in the uprising.

The Celali Revolts were a response to the increasing injustices to the Turkmen people during the Ottoman era. Religion was the traditional value to die for before ideologies, just as ideologies "to die for" were born for rebellion in modernity. In other words, temporal claims and uprisings against injustices were exhausted by using religion as a useful tool.

"... We must now admit that the most unhappy among those subject to these glorious empires were the Anatolian Turks, who constituted the overwhelming majority of the society. Koçi Bey was able to warn the sultan by saying, "How many treacherous and drunken city boys are entering the imperial harem? The Turk, nomad, gipsy, Jewish, and the unfaithful" ("Risale", p.45). The extent of the ruling group's hostility towards and contempt for Turks, pushed a significant part of the population to stand for the Shia, which emphasizes lineage in the sectarian division within Islam.

The Turkmen were always offended and angry with the Seljuks."[81]

The definition of religious-secularist in the class conflict that broke out while the Anatolian bourgeoisie was rising against the republican devshirme bureaucracy is the continuation of this historical trend.[82]

There are certain facts that the Republic inherited from the Ottoman Empire: The old Ottoman bourgeoisie of Muslim and non-Muslim Istanbul shopkeepers and devshirme bureaucrats were in a union of interests against those of the Turkmen periphery. This is why old Istanbulis lamented non-Muslims leaving Istanbul in the Republican era. "Oh where is my Greek, Armenian, Jewish neighbour?" was a sincere lamentation. These complaints were the manifestation of a historical class solidarity reflected in the Republic.

When Turks and Kurds of Anatolia shifted to fill the vacuum non-muslims left in Istanbul, they were met with disgust in the beginning. While the Ottoman devshirme used the word "Etrak-ı bî-idrak" to scorn the Anatolian Turkmen rudely, they were in cooperation with the non-Muslim bourgeois of Istanbul. In this system, Anatolia had to feed the devshirme bureaucrats and non-Muslim bourgeoisie in Istanbul. In times of economic deterioration, devshirme and non-Muslim Constantinople would cooperate in coups. We can

---

[81] Göka, 2006, ibid. p. 183
[82] Göka, 2006, ibid. p. 253

understand this nostalgia for the old bureaucrats of today's Istanbul who are over seventy years old.

Land looting and squatting, which started especially during the Adnan Menderes period, was perhaps the subconscious revenge of the Turkmen on Istanbul, who had been exploited for centuries, by Istanbul. The acceleration of the flow of Anatolian Turkmen in Istanbul after Turgut Ozal naturally disturbed the former residents. What is interesting is how the children of poor people who came from Anatolia and conquered Istanbul, living in slums and how it is reflected in today's social psychology, lifestyle and political preferences. This area too, can be an interesting subject of academic study.

Likewise, there were five historical churches still active in Pera, what Beyoğlu is today, and no mosques. As non-Muslims left, and Muslim Turks live in Beyoğlu today, a sound mind can not understand the opposition of devshirmes for the construction of a mosque in the area for the needs of millions of Muslims. It took the efforts of a century to build the Taksim mosque in Istanbul together with the Istanbul Opera House, facing each other, both jewels erected during AKP rule.

The opposition of a Muslim to the construction of a mosque in Pera for Muslims is also an interesting field for psychological research.

Continuing with our subject, remember the saying:
"Turkmen and the Kurd conquered Istanbul in the second half of the 20th century." They riveted the seals of

conquest with the re-conversion of Hagia Sophia back into a mosque as per Fatih's will, and built Taksim and Çamlıca mosques.

Of course, it is not easy for a Japanese, African or Chilean looking at these matters to understand the irrationality and subconsciousness of the "Muslim" Turks vehemently opposing the Islamization of Pera, which has been a Christian district for centuries but no longer has non-Muslims and the construction of a mosque in its centre. The simple truth is that this job is a manifestation of class conflict. Still, it is an anomaly that will enter the field of research in social psychology.

Before closing this issue, an anecdote: It may be in 1964, we went to the Ministry of Health Heybeliada, (one of the beautiful Prince Islands of Marmara Sea) recreational facilities for a holiday as a family. One day, as we, a few rural youths, went down to the pier, it was full of lively, wealthy Greek youth and no one spoke Turkish. It was as if we were in a foreign land. It is impossible to describe the shock we were in. If the films of those years are remembered, the lifestyle of the cosmopolitan high society of Istanbul, the remnant of the Tanzimat era, will be better understood, while rural primary school students were fed with AID American milk powder in the 1960s. The Ottoman Greeks' desire to return to the Ottoman days, mentioned by Prof. Dr Dimitri Kitsikis, is the expression of such sincere and logical nostalgia.

Suhte Revolts

Just as hungry families saw the church as a door to feed their children in Medieval Europe, rural Turkmen families saw sufi lodges as lifesaving havens for their starving children, especially during the Great Kaçgun period (where public order was destroyed due to hunger, taxes became unbearable, and people left the villages and fled to the mountains. But like today's university graduates, the "suhte"[83] when they finished school, they were unemployed, hungry, and in unrest. Their uprisings were called "religious" uprisings, ignoring their socio-economic roots. Real, active uprisings in the name of religion were coming out at the center when the educated Istanbul ulema were unhappy.

Tanzimat

Let us emphasize one point again. The Empire was a multi-ethnic, multi-religious empire. No group, including the Turkmen, had priority in the eyes of the state. What should the ruling class do when such a state starts collapsing?

In the beginning, a modern Ottomanism that many non-Muslims sincerely also wanted was considered. But

---

[83] Suhte; It is a term used for madrasah students in the Ottomans. The word sûhte, which means "burnt, ignited" in Persian, was used for madrasa students in the Ottoman period, referring to their burning with the love of science. This term took the form of softa over time. TDV Encyclopedia of Islam, Hyperlink: https://bit.ly/3wKJSs0

the nation-state poison triggered by the French Revolution was now inflamed in the Balkans. Next, the rulers wanted to use Islam as a glue, and the wind of separation also swept the Arab lands. Finally the devshirme administration remembered that they were Turks. So came the final verdict. The new state was going to be a Turkish nation-state. A modern State of the Turkmen who founded the Ottoman State. Turkish language was simplified and the intellectual fashion of "going to the people", to the rural Turkmen, began.

Intellectual trials were conducted in the design of the new state. First, to rehabilitate the old. But it turned out that since the Empire could not die when it should have died, it was extremely corrupt and the situation became too dire to be corrected. Next, a complete reset was considered. In other words, everything that was past would be discarded and everything new would be taken from the West. At this point, the "cultural revolution", which was far from reality and caricatured in the novels of the period, started.

Since there was no infrastructure on which to build a culture in the Young Republic, Westernization remained as an imitation at the top, and it did not spread to the rural people, ninety per cent of whom were peasants, still "using the Hittite plow" as İlber Ortaylı said.

However, the initiative took a sick turn. The Arab/Persian cultures, which separated the classical Ottoman devshirme from the Turkmen, this time left their place to the Western culture. The movement towards the people again failed until 15 July 2016.

Let's listen to Prof. Kucukomer on people's answer to the ruling devshirmes who wanted to embrace them after a millennial schism: *"The opposition grew like an avalanche outside the parliament. In fact, freedom immediately brought popular opposition to the bureaucrats."*[84]

---

[84] Küçükömer, ibid. p.86

PART THREE

Early Republic

Now, let's go to the early Republican period. The Ottoman devshirme bureaucrats continued flawlessly and uninterruptedly with the Republic. The Ottoman tradition of educating smart peasant children and sending successful ones to Europe (no nepotism) continued. And these children were meant to be "Cultural Westerners", to be detached from their Anatolian Turkmen families and environment.

İdris Kucukomer: *"There is a kind of "Ottoman feudalism" different from that of the West. Important element in the said Ottoman feudalism was the fief-holding sipahis or the rulers. In short, Ottoman bureaucrats. If a remnant of these is to be sought, it is today's Republican bureaucrats who have serious commonalities with this remnant."*[85]

The monthly dancing balls held in the 1950s at the mess halls of Turkish air bases, and the American cultural islands in rural Türkiye confirm Zafer Toprak's observations on Turkish modernisation. Touring Turkish Air Force Jazz Band was a successful instrument in preparing the forerunners of the "Western lifestyle" in the new Republic.

---

[85] Küçükömer, ibid. p. 135

Idris Kucukomer again: *"Tanzimat... This is also the era of balls. As domestic production was swiftly eroding and unemployment skyrocketing, balls held in the Ottoman embassies, palaces, and European Embassies in Istanbul were in full swing, Ottoman bureaucrats partied together with their Western and Levantine friends. Then come Republican People's Party rule. As Anatolian towns were suffering from shortage of supplies, it was impossible not to notice continuation of the fancy balls in the new Republic as against people's hating eyes."*[86]

An important point; There was a cultural schism between the devshirme bureaucrat of Arab/Persian/Byzantine synthesis, and its counter the peasant Turkmen in Ottoman times. Now, in the modernist Republic, the peasant Turkmen had to face the new, Westernised bureaucrat. Here, too, the term "Turkmen" does not mean a race or ethnicity, but the ruled, the periphery.

Kucukomer: *"The congress held in Paris in 1902 by the bureaucratic Young Turk movement against Sultan Abdulhamid is extremely important. This meeting revealed the core of the dichotomy that has become more evident in Ottoman society, or rather the tendency of schism between Westernist bureaucrats and Islamist-Oriental popular front against them. The struggle shaping the vicious cycle at the top, a schism continuing to our day, and not finding reflection at the grassroots."*[87]

---

[86] Küçükömer, ibid. p. 69
[87] Küçükömer, ibid. p. 79

Indeed, the Young Turks and the other Republican bureaucrats did realise the need to go to the people, and to "bring civilization to the countryside - mission civilisatrice", they had to have a common vocabulary with the people. Thus came the simplification of the Ottoman language. Yet the efforts were fruitless. How could they accept a Turkmen revolution toppling their millennial rule, a "Turkmen coup" that would topple their own class in a somewhat Marxist understanding? To bring about a genuine democratic Anatolian revolution? Idris Kucukomer believed that their only goal was cultural modernization. In any case, neither the population nor the infrastructure was prepared for such revolution, nor was any party yet aware of it.

Class Consciousness - Beginnings of Conflict

Strange enough, it was not the CHP, the champion of Western cultural ideology and comprador of Western "lifestyle", which made Turks materialist. Grassroots modernization had to wait for the second half of the 20th century, with Republic's two pious presidents Turgut Ozal and Recep Tayyip Erdogan, who woke Turkish appetite for material possessions of this world and made Turks materialist.

As industrialization pulled masses into the metropols and 93% of the population became urban, they woke up from the millennial sleep for the afterlife and had started to attack the material goods of THIS WORLD with greed and hunger. Call it Atatürk's Weberian dream?

Democracy and modern cultural development would follow.

A paradox needs attention here. It is the 21st century industrialisation, infrastructure investments and modernization of the AKP, which continued on the path laid by Ozal, that made the people virtually materialistic. But since materialism is a Young Turk ideology — especially of Abdulhamid's students— the votes of materialists go to the CHP, not the AK Party. Why? Because as the continuation of the Young Turk, CHP promises a cosmopolitan "Western lifestyle", including LGBTQ.

In other words, CHP proposes not only the materialist philosophy, but also the alienation of the self from its roots in the devshirme tradition. Aiming for a cultural transformation by completely erasing the past, including authentic tradition, morality and religious understanding. And roughly 1/4 of the population, descendants of the millennially oppressed periphery, enthusiastically embrace this offer.

One of the most crucial research areas facing our nation is "reset," or rejection of the past. Translation of foreign laws, as well as changing bankrupt institutions and concepts, were subjects that the state apparatus discussed in the early days of the Republic. But why do young people today want to run away from who they are? Why do they want to put their past behind? Furthermore, why don't they even want to confront their past?

One-fourth of the population is in self-hatred. To overcome such self-hatred, the first phase should be falling into an identity crisis. Not on the horizon yet. Then would come the search for a modern authentic identity. Again, not yet. Then how to build a new identity? Where is politics in all of this confusion?

Although AKP is the modernising party, it wants to preserve the historical values of Anatolia as much as possible and to use them as shock absorbers against sudden global shocks to balance the materialist culture that it had created. Another fact that requires academic scrutiny.

Going back to history: Celali revolts – the rebellion of the periphery against the ruling Ottoman devshirme class. Though a technical manifestation of Turkmen's resentment born out of economic hardships and oppression, it was defined as a religious war, just like today's rivalry is being distorted as the war of religious fanatics against secular modernists, to be crushed as a "religious" uprising, just like the Celali revolts before.

Küçükömer again:

"The Westernist-secular bureaucrat tries to save the state with Westernization. And Westernization needs economic forces which Turkey of the time did not have. Hence the opposition with the great popular front, leading to a struggle between secular Westerners and religious Easterners. A game in which the civilian and military bureaucrat would supposedly be considered progressive, while the Islamist-Oriental camp, which was

tricked into isolation by bureaucrats in imperialist grip, would be considered reactionary, regressive!"[88]

"In the Second Constitutional Monarchy (1908), we saw the continuation of the rivalry between the people who took refuge in the Islamist circles, versus the secular bureaucrats. We see the same fight in the Republican era. Unfortunately the fight has been seen as a superstructural fight between religious people and the secularists who are called progressive just because they were Westernists. Thus, Türkiye, which was conditioned not to go down to the fundamentals of the contradictions, was divided into two. Only imperialism benefited from this schism. Doesn't it look like that today?[89]

We should add a large part of the military officers to the Westernist-secular bureaucrat group. But these officers so-called intellectuals, could not understand the effects of imperialism on the economy, especially the choking of industry and resulting unemployment. This is why they were unable to establish a real organic connection with the people for their movement, which they called revolution or reform."[90]

"...there seems to be a so-called 'cultural revolution'. Of the existing productive forces and the people, the majority will not be able to accept the elite Cultural Revolution movement (from its constitution to its art) and will even react. We should not be misled by the

---

[88] Küçükömer, ibid. p. 95
[89] Küçükömer, ibid. p. 84
[90] Küçükömer, ibid. p. 93

religious appearance of the reaction. What we must do is to understand the historical truth behind it. We must correctly see the Westernist-laicist bureaucrat's exploitation of such religious appearance for his power."[91]

Back to Erol Goka. *"Celali Revolts and the despotic meaures to extinguish them have never ceased. Actually, as against assertions, their uprisings were not motivated by any form of sectarianism. A report prepared during final years of Magnificient Sulaiman's time, regarded as the height of the Ottoman Empire, noted that desperate Anatolian Turkmens were "eating grass" due to starvation."*[92]

The February 28, 1997 junta generals tagging provincial merchants as green Islamist capital and banning trade with them, while encouraging globalist/cosmopolitan Istanbul capital against the rising rural capital, is a grave continuation of this historical Machiavellian game.

Moreover, Western interests using the expertise of Orientalist academics and experts, are observing Turkish society like a lab bug under a microscope. In the lab, they find two instruments for manipulation. The "religious-laicist fight" and "love/enmity of Atatürk". And they skillfully use these two factors in the historical class warfare of the two classes.

---

[91] Küçükömer, ibid. p. 95
[92] Göka, 2006, ibid. p. 242

The Republican class war seems to have started between the CHP and the DP. This, too, is a misleading image. In reality, the DP is an offshoot of the CHP. Both were established by devshirme cadres. In the 1940s and 1950s, the infrastructure had not been built, and the political lines had not yet been sharpened. At the beginning of the Republic, the ratio of ninety per cent peasant versus ten per cent urban has reversed to ninety-three per cent urban versus seven per cent peasant today, and the masses that have flooded the metropolises have now begun to notice the diversity of interest in the historical ruling class with much clearer lines.

The Free Party, which Atatürk had asked his friend Fethi Okyar to found in 1930, was an experiment that scared the devshirme bureaucrats of the serious potential of provincial threat to their historical rule. The 1950 elections were the last warning to the devshirme bureaucracy.

The "reactionary political Islam" rhetoric classically used by the USA to prevent democratization in Islamic countries today was used in Türkiye against the awakening of the Anatolian Turkmen and formed the so-called "pro-Ataturk" basis of military coups manipulated by the USA.

Academics like Taner Timur, in line with devshirme tradition, describe the current Anatolian Turkmen uprising against Westernist cosmopolitan governments as a "religious-reactionary" counter-revolution to the "cultural revolution" of the Republic.[93]

Whereas for Idris Kucukomer, a bureaucrat was attempting to impose Western institutions, western culture, and Western lifestyle on the populace within the historical Ottoman tradition without offering the general public anything. Theirs were referred to as "revolutions."

In truth, the Western-oriented junta attempt to stop the Anatolian Turkmen from embracing the materialism that Atatürk had imagined was a regressive response. In reality, the West saw its "values and lifestyle" as the "end of history" and imposed them on the global village. Any nation out of their realm was a threat to Western interests. "Those who don't share my values and my way of life are a threat to me." Hence all nations had to be ruled by autocrats educated in the West or Westernised. If not, they were toppled.

The West could not allow the Anatolian populace to overthrow their useful idiots, the "men of the West." Parties of Islamic cultures were a perennial threat to the West. Western media were always ready to demonize parties and politicians of Islamic roots. To sum up, Europe and the United States prevented Muslim countries from democratizing. They also prevented democracy in these nations from developing in their own course and evolving naturally.

---

[93] Taner Timur, "AKP'nin önlenebilir Karşı-Devrimi - Avoidable Counter-Revolution of AKP" 2014

After joining NATO, the Republican devshirme administration adopted a very different stance from that of the romantic, aspiring cultural Westernism of the Tanzimat era. With industrialisation and awakening masses flowing to the metropolises, the country was confronted with a modern class conflict this time.

The Ottoman Empire did not have the capitalist/working classes of industrialization in the Marxist sense, nor the aristocrats versus serfs of feudal Europe. Yet, there were two classes in conflict: The ruling and ruled classes, as Plato had pointed out 2,500 years earlier.

The periphery, which flowed from the rural to the metropolises with its "religion and traditions", could no longer be assimilated into the Western cultural mix, nor could it be allowed to take over the power from the Western comprador administration. In the process, an artificial political separation was created. In the 1970s, peasant students were split into right-wing and left-wing groups and killed each other, while the bureaucratic elite and its Western supporters gained time.

In the early Republic, in its millennial learned helplessness, the peasant, ninety per cent of the population, could not rebel against the devshirme. Forget daring to, they could not even think of preventing the execution of their beloved Prime Minister Adnan Menderes, leaving his neck to his executioner generals.

Looking from a different angle, the execution of a Prime Minister was the continuation of the toppling and execution of Ottoman Sultans and Grand Viziers by unhappy janissaries. According to the Ottoman social contract, the State had to give security and justice to the reaya, and in return, the reaya was never to be engaged in politics and governance. Hence toppling governments and executions were political matters which never were people's business.

And comes urbanization. When people became ninety-three per cent urban, in materialist awakening, they started to go for their political interests. This time to get over their despair. And defy rolling tanks with bare hands.

Bloodless Revolution of the Turk

As experiences of Europe's 1789 (French), 1830 (July), 1848 (February), 1917, and China's 1949 Communist revolution showed, by the late 20th Century, the conflict of the historical ruling class versus emerging new bourgeois in Türkiye was maturing for a bloody showdown. Necmettin Erbakan, leader of the then Islamists, however, prepared the ground for a bloodless revolution thanks to his patience and common sense.

And it was with AKP that the democratic, nonviolent Anatolian Revolution occurred. The army was ordered to its proper barracks. As the Ottoman provincial judges stood up for the locals against the corrupt bureaucracy, the Republican judiciary started to revert to its roots, make peace with the Anatolian values from which they emerged, and act by them. Police were the first in bureaucracy to embrace their roots, and rural Turks welcomed them warmly.

The Republic started with a few universities, castles of Westernization, in three big cities as elite colleges like the Ottoman Enderun, aiming to produce bureaucrats of the new State. With the expansion of 210 universities into rural Anatolia, unassimilated Anatolian academics started to emerge. Old academia of the Ottoman elite Enderun tradition protested the expansion of universities with the pretext that quality was sacrificed in the process. Many academics, feeling cut off from their old elite status, started to leave the country.

In short, through a peaceful revolution, the devshirme bureaucracy and academia ceded its position to the Anatolian Turks.

Founding Father of Turkish Democracy

Erdogan went down in history as the "founding father of Turkish Democracy" with the July 15 Revolution. July 15 is a millennial revolution, the day Turks stopped the Ottoman janissary tradition of toppling and killing rulers.

It is at least as important as the French Revolution. On that day, Turks, under the leadership of Erdogan, declared to the world that they would never, ever again, leave their democratically elected politicians at the mercy of bloody juntas.

It is a great national holiday. At this point, we can express without hesitation, with a sterile view, far above political considerations: British Prime Minister David

Lloyd George said about Atatürk, *"Centuries rarely produce geniuses. Look at our misfortune that the genius of the 20th century was given to the Turks and fate brought him before us."*[94] Just as his word has echoed in history, a similar word will be uttered about Recep Tayyip Erdogan by future historians. Erdogan, who destroyed the thousand-year-old devshirme order that has been ruling since the Seljuks, returned to the Turk, the power to govern.

Beyond emancipating headscarves and abolishing oppression of Muslims, Erdoğan recognized the Kurdish identity, freed Kurdish speech in Türkiye, recognized the rights of the Alevis and "returned their Alevi dede's" despite Atatürk's order: "Some sheikhs, dedes...". He has already made his mark in history as a revolutionary who also recognized and restored the rights of confiscated non-Muslim religious heritage too.

Reactionary Counter-Revolution

The Turkish Revolution of 15 July has been a dark day for the West, which is in the habit of ruling Muslim countries

---

[94] "A mass of voters of low-income or who have made a fortune, who are grossly aware that even though they no longer step on the back of their shoes, they are despised and not accepted by the elite of the society. A mass of voters who express their awareness with their discontent and determine the dynamics of Turkey's new social structure... The Chairman of the Justice and Development Party is a perfect fit, so to speak, in terms of stimulating the hopes and aspirations of this electorate." Nur Vergin, Where Politics and Sociology Meet, Turkey Diary, Spring – 2004, issue 76

with Westernist generals and autocrats. 15 July was the day the West and its Westernist representatives tried a final "REGRESSIVE COUNTER REVOLUTION" against the millennial popular revolution of the Turkmen. Just to remind you, junta members, who have killed 250 innocent humans and bombed the National Congress, Presidential Palace and the Ministry of Defence are protected in the USA, Germany, Greece and other NATO countries! Fact!

Counter-revolution was indeed both real and bloody. The urbanized people had left their learned helplessness behind. Their message was clear. After that night, any devshirme junta which was planning a coup had to risk a bloody, massive public reaction. Erdogan's charisma created millions of brave people who would die for him should a junta attempt to kill him.

Interestingly, CHP, the representative political party of the bankrupt devshirme bureaucracy, wanted the wounded July 15 veterans to be prosecuted for opposing the junta coup. Fact! In other words, it was a warning that Anatolian Turks should not oppose the coups of the military/bureaucrat devshirme class. After a while, the CHP began not to celebrate the July 15 Democracy Days. Because July 15 was a real popular revolution that overthrew the historical, archaic class represented by the CHP. As we said earlier, CHP is the political and cultural successor of the Tanzimat and Union and Progress cadres.

In short, the date of 15 July 2016 can be commemorated as the birthday of Turkish democracy and people's power. It can be considered as the collapse of the millennial oligarchic, alien, devshirme class. Let us repeat, July 15, 2016, is the birthday of Turkish Democracy. From now on, every putschist has to start by knowing that the coup will be bloody and that the people will protect the leader they chose democratically.

To put it straight, starting with the Tulip Era of the 18th century, continuing with the Tanzimat and the early Republic, it was clear that monkeying Western culture and alienation from roots was not a revolution. The accusation of religious reaction, bigotry, and counter-revolutionary stance ascribed to the Anatolian people (including our Alevis) turned out to be empty rhetoric. Revolution in the sense of class warfare is the overthrow of the thousand-year-old devshirme rule by the Anatolian Turkmen. The reactionary counter-revolution, on the other hand, is the effort of Westernist juntas to take back the power from the Anatolian Turkmen.

In this sense, a note, far above the daily politics: Tayyip Erdogan has taken his place in history as the Founding Father of the Turkmen government and democracy. In a sense, he realized Atatürk's dream.

Turkmen to the Mission

In the beginning, we said Turkmen was the core who founded the Seljuk and Ottoman Empires. Then we said that the Turkmen were excluded from the administration. Let's be fair, it was the Ottoman devshirme bureaucrats who founded the Republic and were the only educated elite to do so. The anthem of Mülkiye, the faculty of political sciences, which I am honoured to have been a lecturer, is "O motherland, let your tears rest because we have grown up". It dates back to 1918, wartime. Gallipoli Defense of WW I, is referred to as "the war of High School teenagers", and the Sakarya Battle is referred to as the "Officers' War".

Yet the hope and self-confidence that came with the victory did not last long. With the early death of Atatürk, cautious, reactive, defensive reflexes resumed encapsulating Turkish politics and bureaucracy. World War II also had an effect in cautious politics which postponed Anatolian takeover. The core Turkmen who founded the Ottomans and Seljuks came belatedly with the July 15, 2016 Revolution, not to hand over their power back to the devshirme.

What might have occurred if the Turkmen had not seized power?

Devshirme bureaucrats indeed founded the young Republic. Apart from Ataturk, they were the bureaucrats still in the defensive mood of Ottoman diplomacy. Against the West, they were still apologetic and passive. Some were proposing an American mandate during the salvation war. Many among them still feared policies that would have annoyed the West. In such a defensive, apologetic spirit, Ottoman decomposition may have continued in the Republic.

We see the same spirit in contemporary politics in the statements of some politicians in need of praise from

Western countries.[95] On the other hand, Anatolian Turkmen hailed in from the exclusion of centuries and were ready to take over the state with a brand new, dynamic spirit. It was indeed Atatürk who ignited this spirit. With his death, Anatolian Turkmen rule was delayed. In the early 21st century, Turkmen took over their state back again, this time to stay. Call of duty after six Centuries. Turkmen waking up to this world with new energy, put the new Republic on the rise.

Behind the Anatolian victory, to repeat, there is a serious factor that is hardly noticed. Ottoman rule was of a twin; the Sultan and his Devshirmes. Sultan was the brain and Devshirmes were the body. By abolishing the Ottoman dynasty, Atatürk destroyed the head of Devshirmes and turned the devshirmes into a rooster without a head. So as long as Ataturk and his successor İnönü ruled, bureaucrats did not feel the loss. With military coups, the last of which was intended on 15 July 2016, they tried to cling to their historical power, and without a head, lost in the end.

Yes, the class war has been won, and transformation has been accomplished. Now it's time for the "Great Jihad". What is Turkmen's great jihad? Starting from its own millennial civilization, it is to create a brand new Turkish synthesis, "Turkish Modernity". Such synthesis, starting with Anatolian values, has to include the

---

[95] Ali Babacan said, "I told the Spanish newspaper all of the things here. They said, 'Isn't it hard?' I said, 'It's hard, but we'll do it'. They will also look from Europe and say with admiration, 'Well done' to Turkey. They'll say, 'Look at that'. Yeni Şafak Newspaper, February 2, 2023.

Western and other civilisations of the global family. With its historical antecedent, the only appropriate choice for an expanding, global civilisation to be.

To start with, useful parts of Western Civilization must be adopted. Then its wrongs, such as its genocides and inability to survive in harmony with other civilisations, its efforts to impose its values and lifestyle to all nations of the world, to be discarded.

Historically Islam and its under branch Turkish Civilisation indeed had the philosophy of live and let live with other civilisations. Within such spirit, it is so easy for them to adopt and engage good parts of the Western civilisation together with those of the other civilisations of humanity to create an embracing new universal civilisation for the new Turkish Century. One may ask why? History is the witness. We did it before, we are among the most eligible to do it again. West failed to create an embracing civilisation. In fact, we shall indeed benefit from Jared Diamond, Ian Morris, Niall Ferguson, Felipe Fernandez Armesto, Samuel Huntington, Francis Fukuyama etc. in taking lessons from the wrongs and goods of the Western civilisation.

We are talking about a peaceful worldview that will rival the declining European concept of the nation-state and capitalist philosophy. We should be able to make far superior assessments and synthesis attempts on questions of why we lagged behind and how we can surpass others, without being destructive. And I have unwavering faith the Turk can do it.

Bourgeoisie

Erol Göka again:

"Since the time we made Anatolia our homeland, we have been trying to settle, urbanize, islamize, and finally modernize. But even a glance at the post-Republican population and settlement movements in Türkiye will suffice to see that the process has not yet been completed in terms of the transformation from nomadism into sedentary, urban lifestyle and that our society has many years ahead to become a modern, urban society." [96]

Since the latest statistics show that we are 93 per cent urban now, and the remaining 7 per cent village population is exposed to the same salvo of television and internet as in the city, and media having broken the peasant isolation, we are faced with a brand new social structure now.

In the classical approach, the village is static, a centre of peace, predictability and stability guaranteed by a culture and common sense distilled through millenia. It is a shock absorber and softener against volatile turbulences of cosmopolitan metropolises.

Elaborating on transition, it is useful to record Erol Güngör's views on the importance of customs and traditions in human societies.

"Although it is slow in some and fast in others, customs and traditions change in every society. In fact,

---

[96] Göka, 2012, ibid. p. 40

their easy and quick change is not good for society. First of all, easy and fast-changing behaviour codes cannot be considered custom or tradition. The survival and continuation of society depends on the existence of common behaviour codes among people. Since customs and traditions meet this need, they form the basis of society. Without them, we would have to rethink how we would behave in every next situation we encounter, and we would never be able to predict how others would behave in varying situations. People would not be able to live as a society in the absence of such common and permanent codes of behaviour among them ..."[97]

Then the obvious question: What serves as the country's "shock absorber" if there are no villages or peasants anymore? When the common sense that the village has filtered through thousands of years disappears in a few generations, what is the "regulator" that will calm social storms? Two most important characteristics of the village are religion and tradition. Both quickly deteriorate in the city, losing their relevance in a few generations. At the metropol, what will replace these two pillars that uphold law and order in the village and act as a unifying force?

The city is temporal. The village was spiritual. Leaving the spiritual lifestyle behind, the West had to build a new code of non-religious materialist morality for this world. The technological revolution, surplus income from imperialism and distribution of welfare to social masses helped the Western society build its positivist

---

[97] Güngör, Ahlak Psikolojisi ve Sosyal Ahlak 1998 p. 96

code of modern ethics. In the 21st century, the advantages of the Western world are challenged by new rising powers, and we are not sure whether modern Western ethics can be instrumental in times of comparative economic decline. It has not yet been put to a stress test.

The questions are the same for the Turk transforming from spiritual to Kantian ethics. In this process, what should be the modern glue, common values and interests that will keep future Turkish generations, the future bourgeoisie safe from disintegration and live in peace? Religion? Tradition? Kantian ethics? What does homeland mean? What do you mean when you say flag? For which common values or interests would you be able to motivate your youth to martyrdom? How will our education system, which alienates young people from their origins with the devshirme tradition, produce answers to these questions?

Religions have been the subject of psychological and sociopolitical debate for centuries. But the most overlooked function of religions is that they are the essence of "identity". Even for an atheist Turkish ruler, the question is valid: What if I remove Islam from Turkish identity? Academic scenarios can be studied. An atheist Türkiye? A Christian Türkiye? A shamanistic Türkiye? This question can be asked of any nation. For example, it is a fact that Atatürk won the War of Independence with the believers who rushed to martyrdom saying "Allah, Allah". So did Turkish NATO soldiers in Korean War as well. With what non-religious motives would we win the war? A statesman, even if he is an atheist, has to keep alive the common values that hold the society together. He cannot attack the values of the society with childlike reactions. No power can annihilate millennial values overnight, and neither can it create new values overnight. Especially if you attack existing values before a new one is formed, you will shatter the society.

And our poor masses...

How can you ensure their happiness in poverty and keep them away from rebellion? Addressing a question, one of the February 28, 1997 junta rebel generals, Çevik Bir, claimed that their will would soften if they sought the advice of sociologists. He did not need science in his narrow, naïve world.

He never realized that the Imam-Hatip schools and the headscarf were then useful transitional tools that Anatolian Turks discovered with a thousand years of common sense. As American journalist Robert Kaplan describes in his famous book *Ends of the Earth,* while all shantytowns around the world were swamps of prostitution, drugs, and murder, those in Türkiye were places of calm and tranquility – clean, quiet homes that cannot be entered with shoes. "Pious, safe, noble, clean". "Houses that smell clean and where there is no crime."

Residents of those slums, with their millennial wisdom, found a practical shock absorber in their transition from village to metropolitan lifestyle, the government İmam Hatip (preacher) schools. In doing so, their intention was not to have imam children. The practical expectation was that those schools would protect their kids from the cultural shock of the city and the vices of cosmopolitan metropolitan lifestyle.

As we said earlier, at the metropol, religion and tradition fade swiftly, creating a sudden ethical void. And a new, modern, secular code of ethics needs at least five generations to settle in. What we have in the process is the lumpen generations in confusion and psychological insecurity. Sending kids to religious schools, and women covering their heads with headscarves were all precautions of millennial wisdom to meet the sudden shocks of modernity in transition.

In fact, it is impossible to escape from modernity in the global village. I saw an interesting example of this with a sterile observation on my trip to Kuala Lumpur in 2000. When I looked through the window of the hotel I was staying at, I saw a young girl in tight stretch blue jeans and a transparent, short-sleeved blouse that showed the bra inside, but with a hijab on her head. Seeing that, I said to myself, "Türkiye in ten years" and murmured, "Bourgeois Islam." Years later, in a television program in Türkiye, when I conveyed my observation that the number of make-up wearers increased among our devout ladies, a politician from the late Erbakan era said, "You cannot divide Islam into country Islam and urban Islam. There is only one Islam." Yes, Islam was one. The Weberian question was how the "urbanized" interpreted and lived Islam. It was how quickly modernity and materialist consumption engulfed our devout bourgeois. Yes, modernity shall swallow the metropolitan, modern Muslim. And the emerging

Muslim urban-dwellers shall create their own Turkish modernity through evolution (not enforced, imposed revolution from the top), digesting global modern values and merging them with their historical values. They will indeed start watching operas. And other high tastes too, shall soon be their lifestyles in a natural way. It already started anyway. Note! Turks did not start enjoying operas and Western classical music because it was imposed on the rural peasants with a revolutionary understanding. They learned to enjoy them because of the gradual urbanization and modernisation. "Lifestyles" evolve gradually.

Modern Politics

Let's now examine why the AKP, in the tradition of the Democratic Party, keeps receiving the majority of the votes from our poor masses, while only a small percentage vote for CHP, the representative of bureaucracy.

Balkan and Arab peoples did not experience the same problems as Turkmen and Alevis during the Ottoman era. Contrary to claims that Turkmen revolts were made by religious heretics, the Celali and Suhte uprisings were social uprisings against political corruption and the deterioration of the economic order.

People with a basic understanding of history will acknowledge that the democratic uprising of the Anatolian people today against the military-civilian bureaucracy is, just like in the past, a conflict between the ruling center and the periphery with roots in socioeconomic problems. In history, the rhetoric was the heretics. Alarm bells rang to save the caliph sultan from heretic uprisings. In the Republic, this time, the rhetoric, "saving Atatürk's secular Republic."

Any intellectual who could comprehend his aspirations would know that Atatürk was with the periphery, with the Anatolian Turks, rather than with the devshirme rulers. It should not be forgotten that as soon as Atatürk closed his eyes, the devshirme Unionists resumed their historical role that had been suspended during Atatürk's time.

Taking the opportunity, it would be helpful to briefly discuss the Celali and Suhte uprisings against the devshirme government.

As feudal Europe was living its Middle Ages with internal strifes, Ottoman Empire was expanding. Turkmen were migrating from Asia to the Balkans, janissaries were engaged in conquests, and the Empire was experiencing a boom in economic activity.

Suleiman the Magnificent's rule, however, marked the beginning of warning signs in the budgets. Within thirty years of Suleiman's passing, social unrest started as a result of the end of conquests and the loss of income from conquests. Pay cuts for the Janissaries led to coups, corruption in the military, and eventually oppression and heavy taxation of the periphery, the Anatolian Turkmen populace.

Come Machiavelli's counsel: "Should the subjects, or the army be satisfied in difficult economic times?" Of course the army was the automatic response to the query. The sultans were now at the mercy of the army thanks to Fatih's devshirme system. Similarly, Istanbul's economy received much higher priority than the provinces. Devshirme janissaries, the bureaucracy, and Istanbul merchants were exempt from paying taxes, while Turkmen suffered heavy taxes. Additionally, the order was broken, the timars that had been given to the Turkmen sipahis in the rising age were now given to Istanbul bureaucrats and janissaries, and as a result, discontent led to an increase in Turkmen rebellions.

The focus was on Istanbul and the Balkans as the empire developed mainly into a Balkan state. More importantly, the devshirme slave rulers were never embraced by Anatolian Turkmen or Turkmen aristocratic families. There was mutual distrust and abhorrence between the two. Due to this, the Balkan uprisings in the 16th and 17th centuries were not as violent as the Anatolian uprisings. The Arab regions of the empire were not as unsatisfied as the Anatolian Turkmen, either. And their uprisings were not as violent as the Anatolian Turkmen's response.

As conquests ended, economic conditions worsened, and corruption rocketed; heavy taxation forced peasants to either migrate to major cities, overcrowding them, or escape to the mountains. Commanders in the periphery began to organize gangs of unemployed youth as bandits, first for self-defense and later for banditry. The atmosphere was ripe for Celali Revolt. As already pointed out, poor Christians of Europe sent their hungry kids to churches, poor Turkmens sent their children to religious lodges to be fed, and the unemployed, religious student graduates began to band together and organize Suhte Rebellions.

As a result, Anatolia lost order, agriculture collapsed during the "Great Escape - from villages" period, taxes decreased, and the state's economic crisis fueled the devshirme rulers' growing corruption. The non-Muslim slave system collapsed after the reign of Murad III, who started incorporating Turkmens into the janissary corps, and then during the reign of Mahmud II (who abolished janissaries in the 19th Century), the inflated janissary numbers reached 300,000.

On the other hand, the main Ottoman army, Anatolian Sipahi System, was weakened as the effective 'timar-fief' system maintaining them was ruined, leaving its place to feudalism. Prof. Halil Inalcik says: *"The Ottoman Empire rose by defeating feudalism, and fell when feudalism defeated it."*

Here, the strengthening of the regional notables in the 18th century may have led the way to an Ottoman aristocracy and bourgeois class. Ottoman Neo-feudalism was not, however, conducive to a European style of modernity. Ottoman state philosophy was not eligible for transformation from an economy of conquest and agriculture to a modern economy. In other words, the devshirme class was unmatched until the AKP era in the 21st century.

Historically the Eastern region of the empire, Kurdistan, which was typically mountainous, was an exception to the system. Of no particular economic value, Ottomans purposefully left the region to a feudal administration of its lords. Republic, empowered by means of modernity, plus the terrorist organization PKK upset the feudal order in the region, a chaotic transformation led to instability and the region became vulnerable to foreign manipulations.

In conclusion, AKP led a democratic revolution that brought the millennial periphery to the centre and overthrew the devshirme military-bureaucrat administration. In the twenty years of its reign, it has established its own bureaucracy sharing its own values. Now alienated devshirme bureaucrat is gone, CHP has lost the class it has been representing. Can CHP depend on the big Istanbul capital which was the second leg it stood on? Not much chance as AKP evolves into a Muslim Liberal Party of Türkiye and Istanbul capital changing course and blinking eye to the AKP. In such outlook, we may say CHP is now an anachronic political entity without a base to represent, without a mission.

Küçükömer again:

"Ismet Pasha (Second President, succeeding Atatürk), the final bureaucrat to the left of the center, correctly realised the necessity of a political coalition of Turkish Bureaucracy with both domestic and foreign capital, for balance and peace in the country. In countries like ours,

some think of these bureaucrats still having relevance in historical state apparatus."[98]

As already mentioned, historical discord exists between the devshirme representative CHP and the Turkmen periphery. This discord also involves Kurdish and Alevi history against Ottoman devshirme rule. The intriguing question is how the Devshirme-Alevi dispute, which had a significant impact on Ottoman history, changed into the Devshirme-Alevi alliance in the Republic. Why, despite historical evidence to the contrary, do some rural Turkmen, Kurds, and Alevis support CHP?

At this point, we may surmise that the classical Young Turk message of CHP, the Western secular lifestyle and modernity against Sunni practices, appeals especially to Alevi masses who have been discriminated against by historical Sunni devshirme rule. Ottoman Sunni oppression versus the Republican secular worldview. Such a worldview has also appealed to the awakened lumpen masses thirsty for material possessions and open to materialism. It is natural that the Western world and its powerful local compradors will use all available resources to support this message.

Let's make a prediction for Turkish politics in the future. The AKP is evolving to modernity in a similar trend as European Christian Democrats. However, the left is bare. In actuality, the AKP's social policies fill that gap. As so-called Anatolian Tigers, businessmen of the

---

[98] Küçükömer, ibid. p. 160

periphery open to global commerce, and seek sync with İstanbul and global big capital, and as AKP starts blinking an eye to this sync, we may head for a conjecture. AKP, like European Christian Democrats, may proceed to become the capital friendly liberal right party of Türkiye.

And the candidate for the left? Of the have-nots? The great, century-old political joke of Türkiye was the pretence of CHP to be the party of the oppressed against the ruling devshirme elite and İstanbul capital. In its historical Young Turk mission and world outlook, it was so alienated from the culture, the religious understanding and traditions of the masses, that it was impossible to be the representative of its historical "other", the underdog.

If not AKP, if not CHP, who is the candidate? Let us do some social engineering here. Logic says the Turkish left shall have to share the values and traditions of the underdog, including Islamic colors. Meaning? Probable fission in the AKP. Like Demokrat Parti of the 1940s budding off from its mother CHP, the potential Muslim Left Party may bud off of AKP after the last term of Recep Tayyip Erdoğan as President. Devout and impoverished Muslims who could not share the benefits that AKP new business enjoyed, may opt for a new party. Or else Yeniden Refah Parti of Necmeddin Erbakan's son Dr Fatih Erbakan may opt for such a mission, inviting the unhappy politicians of AKP and its voters too after Erdoğan. And if they can succeed, they would be my future preference.

Those who do not establish roots in "people's" values become rootless and would lose their mission. Turkish left must therefore respect the common values of the populace. A historical lesson of Turkish democracy, the Turkish Left of the 1960s had no shared values with the oppressed it claimed to represent. And paid dearly for their estrangement from the realities of Türkiye.

To say again, in the near future, the rising Anatolian capital and the capital of Istanbul may come to an understanding on a reasonable point and enter into a union of interests. Against these two main parties, the HDP or a successor party representing one part of the Kurdish population, will continue to exist as the reality of Türkiye.

As for the CHP... Although the historical devshirme it represented has disappeared, it is possible and beneficial for this party to continue with a ten per cent vote rate, with the memory of a thousand years of nostalgia and genes of statehood.

The USA - Catalyst of the Turkish Democratic Revolution

The USA, as we previously stated, meticulously studies its target nations like insects under a microscope. The world's top universities, specialists, and intelligence analysts all hail from the United States. But the executive decisions are made by the politicians. And politicians make mistakes. And as Joe Biden confessed, they made a grave strategic error in the "Grand Plan" to topple AKP from power. They never calculated the unintended consequences of failure.

To start with, the USA, with great accuracy, saw the Achilles heel of Turkish society and worked on the historical political schism between the ruling devshirmes and the ruled. As we said above, for devshirme bureaucrats, conservative parties were the Islamist religious fanatics who were the enemies of Ataturk's revolutions. And the USA figured out that pious Muslims needed a saviour from the oppressing laicist bureaucracy. And FETÖ was the most successful operation in the USA. When the July 15, 2016, unsuccessful military coup came, it was too late. Yes, the coup was the result of the most successful intelligence operation in human history. But luckily, it failed.

And the unintended consequence: Even the best minds of the USA could not calculate that the failed coup d'etat would lead to a democratic revolution that would end the thousand-year-old devshirme regime.

They never thought that they would trigger a popular revolt that would route the generals to their barracks forever and that they would never dare stage a coup again.

The USA, which expertly manipulated Atatürk and laicism in the devshirme military-civilian administration, failed at one point and unintentionally sparked the "Turkish Democratic Revolution." Due to this revolution, the army was forced to retreat to its barracks, and the populace vowed to shed blood in order to ensure that juntas were never allowed to control the governments they chose anymore. And Turkish history opened a bright new page after closing the thousand-year-old "Devshirme" story.

This was a millennial, historical revolution, and a real celebration. This was the end of a millennium of military-bureaucratic rule. And it was the USA that triggered it.

Presidential System

The symbolic president. A constitutional sultan. When Atatürk overthrew the sultan, the devshirme bureaucracy became like a rooster with its head severed. After Atatürk, they made an effort to hold onto power with" National Chief" İsmet İnönü, later with Presidents from military juntas. Fake sultan presidents could not succeed. A soldier gets his stars by deference and getting orders. If such a formatted man becomes the autocrat, who shall he turn to get orders? Many junta leaders got their orders from the USA.

In the old system, the USA could blackmail or intimidate a few generals or party leaders behind closed doors to elect the man they wanted as president. A President elected by a few to be intimidated or bought? Versus a President directly elected by the people. A politician tested through decades, and known even to his private psychological details. Whether he is intelligent or mentally ill, democracy allows the public to know him.

Turkish voters, with the exception of a few, never knew the Presidents who were elected by their representatives in the parliament. With Erdogan elected directly by the grassroots, we now have a precise example of clashing interests. Biden, in his TV interview, realising he is not able to topple him, says he wants to bring Erdoğan down in a democratic way by supporting the opposition. But he does not want Russia or China to do the same to the USA... If Erdoğan was to be elected by the parliament, other manipulations to block him, as in the past, may have been available. That is why we see the American and European press and the elite's cry for a parliamentary system in Türkiye.

Now, let us talk about the evolution of European democracy: Feudal lords, the Vatican, and Kings. Checks and balances of the three contending powers. Then comes capitalism, followed by social justice, the agreement to divide the excess profits that the capitalists make from global exploitation with the working class. Then duel for the colonies, and the suicide of Western Civilisation with two ruthless world wars.

Then comes fatigue and the culture of reconciliation as European nations grew weary of fighting one another. Wisdom gained through perpetual warfare. Come political culture of conciliation and coalitions.

Turkish democratic process: Hailing from Ottoman tradition, strict political centralism. Celali revolts aside. The state is the despotic father; ethnic and religious groups are like children cohabiting peacefully with the fear of their despotic father, never maturing to learn the politics of how to bargain and reconcile when the authority is absent. No culture of political consensus. Hence, there is a natural need for "leader" based politics. Party leaders could not be "primus inter pares". They could not be replaced; they were elected for life. Lifelong leadership in all fields. Worker unions, commercial and industrial chambers, political parties, civil society groups, and the like.

Success and prosperity in politics depend on loyalty rather than merit. Party leaders appoint possible deputies and place them into electable positions in elections. After elections, those deputies elect the party leaders who appointed them. In such a parliamentary system of appointed deputies, they raise their hands when ordered to do so.

Then comes the presidential system, where the cabinet is appointed by the president, not from deputies, but like the American technocratic presidential Secretaries of the State, loyal to the president. And the door opened for a Parliament to evolve into an organ of deputies with more liberty to control and impose their free will on the Presidential government.

Republic: The father figure state continues during the time of Atatürk and his successor İnönü. 1950 elections. A test of political bargaining and reconciliation between devshirmes and awakening periphery. Failure. America instigated a military coup in 1960. Prime Minister Menderes and two Ministers were hanged. Janissary tradition continues. To control the democratically elected parliament, the Constitutional

Court was founded. High Administrative Court empowered to control Governments. Justice mechanism, a historical branch of devshirme bureaucracy, not protecting people's rights against the state, but of the state against the grassroots.

Generals realised they could not force people to vote for their representative CHP, hence the era of coalitions. Years of social and economic unrest... Military coups every ten years. Then in the 21st century comes AKP. The constitution was changed to a presidential system. The nation experiences a period of stability, every sector of the economy experiences rapid growth. Infrastructure accomplished. The Republic enters a new age of modernity.

If we go back to the Ottoman system, the sultan and the devshirme bureaucracy dominate the political system. Ottoman Political Contract with Reaya: "I will give you justice and security. I will not interfere with your lifestyle, no matter what your religion or disposition is. And you will not get involved in politics."

Yet the Turkmen is unruly. The tension between Turkmen and devshirme is the reality of Ottoman political history. There are no feudal lords or Vatican-type free clergy in between, forcing the central authority to a culture of political consensus. The people are so politically worthless in the eyes of the state that it was not even necessary to seek reconciliation with them. Political culture has never been developed among the people, so there is a grassroots[99] consensus.

In a society where there is no culture of political consensus, the success of coalition governments is an illusion, even oblivion. The Turkish people, with common sense, have decided on the Presidential System, which conforms to their own character and is commanded by their political culture, which has continued since the Ottoman Empire. This is what fits the nature of things, and with this system, the country has stabilised and made great leaps forward.

Is the establishment of a culture of political consensus in Türkiye a dream? Is the practice of European coalitions a good thing? Can the Western world maintain a culture of compromise and coalition if it loses wealth? Can the Turkish commercial bourgeoisie develop, gain a "win-win" consensus culture between businessmen and the public and reflect it in politics? It is possible. However, it is doubtful whether the coalition power can prevail over the Presidential System, which hails from a thousand-year-old tradition.

Changing Roles

In the 1940s and 50s, the teacher at the school, the commander in the military, the police at the police station, and the doctor in the hospital used to beat ordinary citizens. The Ottoman saying for the parents

---

[99] Grassroots: A movement that arises spontaneously, unorganized, from the bottom up.

who gave their children to the school would say, "His flesh is yours, bones are mine". Parents give teachers a blank check to beat their kids to educate them. Bastinado was also used as a training method for unruly kids. Such violence continuing in many fields in the early Republic, was considered very normal in those days. Acceptance of violence by the peasantry was the result of the "learned helplessness" of the peasants against the bureaucrats who were "recruited from their very village."

Come 21st century, 93% of the population is urban. First modernisation starts in police organisation. A revolution in the field of human rights started in Türkiye with the abolition of torture in police stations and the right to call a lawyer immediately with the Transparent Police Station.

In line with urbanisation, compulsory military service, conditioning the peasant to fear the state by the military, ends. Armed Forces start hiring permanent soldiers on salary, and compulsory service turns into a short voluntary one for a certain fee.

As a police grandson, I can say that centuries-old practice did not disappear overnight. The police, who made the thief talk by beating him and warning him: "Do not fall into my hands again," so that he would not steal again, showed his reaction against the new laws by being offended, "How will this work without beating?" It took a long time for Turkish police to learn modern security techniques. Today's police organisation has proven itself in terms of democratic and humane methods. We can claim that Turkish police are more conscientious and more humane than many Western countries, including the USA. We're talking about a cop who doesn't draw a gun even when some bully punches him!

Another characteristic of the Turkish police is that, despite being one of the main actors in the exercise of state power, it is the bureaucrat class that is most accessible to the general public. Culturally, it has never broken away from the values of its roots, has never been alienated, and has always been intertwined with its people. Police College has never been a devshirme school like military, political science and medical schools. For this reason, it has been the forerunner in modern times of the fusion of the people and the state, and the people have quickly embraced the humanitarian police with full heart.

It takes a much longer time for the other bureaucratic institutions to approach the concept of human rights. The young bureaucrat sitting on the other side of the table continues to see himself above the people he came from, with a historical reflex.

93% urban today, the villagers' ingrained helplessness and fear vanish, even being replaced by the urge to exact revenge on bureaucracy for its historical sins. The clearest illustration of this can be found in hospitals. The young government doctor still uses the familiar pronoun "singular you – sen" when speaking to the elderly patient, seemingly unaware of the fact that he is a servant of the taxpayer. Yet, on the other hand, the peasants broke from state fear, but had not yet attained the level of bourgeois respect for one another and, without manners, used unacceptable, even criminal assaults on doctors. Both parties need to learn to respect each other in a short time.

Before closing the issue, it is useful to mention white-collar lumpens working in areas where there is high demand in the private sector. They can also enter the commanding psychology of government officials when they have authority. Capitalism mandates that satisfying the customer is essential for sales. With this obligation, they will soon learn to respect "humans" the hard way. Because if the company loses customers, they will be kicked out the door. Nowadays, big companies, as well as many government services, follow up with their employees by asking customers whether they got good service from their servants. Turkish society is in swift transformation in human rights.

The Unclaimed State

"Regardless of what anyone says, the Republic is undoubtedly a revolution in Turkish history. With the Republic, Turks turned for the first time towards a civilisational objective that emphasises equality and solidarity not only for themselves but also for everyone with whom they share a common world. We must, therefore have more deliberation on "Turkish modernisation".[100]

Currently, our nation is going through a very delicate transition. As the state transitions to new ownership,

---

[100] Göka, 2006, ibid. p. 184

historical class conflict causes significant harm to the state. The rising Anatolian bourgeoisie, with the first revolution of the new millennium, seized control of the state from the devshirme bureaucracy.

With a sense of victorious confidence, yet with some psychology of historical inferiority, the Turkmen approach the defeated devshirme with tolerance. On the other hand, the devshirmes, in a psychology of defeat, are in a fierce assault against the victors. They mock and insult the emerging Anatolian bourgeois, their lifestyle and cultural differences. Natural human reactions for psychiatrists to work on.

Yet, we should also beware of a potential backlash. Victory fosters generosity, and those who seize control of the state exhibit this maturity. However, it is also possible that some among the victors may act with a spirit of millennial vengeance. The real threat to our sense of national unity may come from feelings of vindictiveness, accusations and denigration of the Westernised devshirmes for being rootless aliens.

Let's now discuss Prof. Vamik Volkan's expertise on social trauma as a result of victimisation.[101]

---

[101] Vamik Volkan, Societal well-being after experiencing trauma at the hand of "Others": The intertwining of political, economic and other visible factors with hidden psychological processes affecting victimized populations. Second OECD World Forum on Statistics, Knowledge and Policy Measuring and Fostering the Progress of Societies, Istanbul, 27-30 June, 2007

Vamik Volkan starts the subject with the concept of "basic trust". He tells about the child's trust in his caregiver, and then this trust develops with the environment and turns into self-confidence. He explains that the trauma of victimisation, on the other hand, is that the sense of trust is destroyed by heavy pains that the individual or society cannot cope with, and that the repair will be "mourning", that is, by revealing and confronting the pain rather than confining it to the depth of the soul. He says that if the psychological poison is not brought to light and spilt, unresolved, unhealed traumas are passed on from generation to generation, and that it is difficult to achieve social peace without understanding and to resolve the hidden psychological processes of societies inheriting trauma.

The legacy of apartheid in South Africa depicts black children adjusting to "Continuous Trauma" and accepting their fate, while adults turn their uncontrollable feelings of despair and retaliation onto themselves. This example may help us understand the lumpen's self-hatred and his desire to identify with his historical oppressors and join them.

It would be worthwhile to examine Reâyâ's historical sufferings, inherited by the Republic's peasants, in light of Volkan's method. Perhaps conditions may be created for the victimised Turkmen, Kurds, Alevis, and pious Muslims to grieve. It might be helpful to bring the subconscious poison of the populace to daylight and alleviate it.

Likewise, the devshirme who lost his throne with the Anatolian Revolution must also mourn, because losing his millennial power is an even more severe trauma. The time has come for these issues to be seriously studied by our social psychologists and psychiatrists. Society will not find peace unless the toxic feelings that have been suppressed in psychological depths are brought to light and healed.

There is reason to be optimistic about social peace. We said that the rising Anatolian bourgeois will create its own modernity. Turkish modernity, which will rise from Anatolian culture, will become natural and mature over time; aspirants to West and Western clones will gradually get rid of the losers' complex and integrate into Turkish modernity. They will also start enjoying and sharing Turkish successes in every field with their compatriots.

In short, they will return to their roots, and the schizophrenic social structure will start healing. In the new Turkish modernity, the ruler and the ruled, devshirme and reaya, will unite in common values and social peace will be established. In that environment, there will be no need for the victorious Turkmen's hostility to the devshirmes they defeated.

Nevzat Tarhan offers some advice for the perilous situation we are in:

"Schizophrenia is a condition in which certain region of the human brain functions differently from another part. Same with a society where one group pursues certain goals and the other part pursues different

goals. Hence harmony in such society is disturbed and social schizophrenia settles in. Social schizophrenia is a feeling that can be taught. Just as clash of a person's feelings and ideas lead to schizophrenia, social schizophrenia occurs when different cultural identities clash in a given society."[102]

A further point was made by Hayrettin Karaman to the effect that our differences should be the factors of unity rather than being divisive. *"When social variation departs from its meaning of wealth, colors of beauty, the drives of the race for perfection, and the means of solidarity, and turn into walls dividing the society, it threatens the unity and integrity of the society, ending in the risk of the nation deteriorating, going backwards, and becoming divided."*[103]

While at the beginning of the Republic the Turkmen used to say, "The state is the state of the beyzades – children of devshirmes", after the July 15 Revolution, it was the devshirme who lamented: "The state is gone, Islamist fanatics have taken over the state". Behind the public rhetoric "We are a country of traitors", we can perhaps look for the violence of class hatred: "If the state is not mine, let it be demolished", "Instead of Enver Pasha's soldiers entering Edirne, let Bulgarian enemy enter it". We can easily understand the alienation and resentment of the devshirme losing power to the Turkmen, seeing they have no projects, dreams or ideals

---

[102] Nevzat Tarhan, Toplum Psikolojisi ve Empati, TİMAŞ Publishing, Istanbul, 2019, p. 36

[103] Hayrettin Karaman - Farklılaşma, parçalanma ve uzlaşma üzerine Yeni Şafak, 27 Kasım 2022

for Türkiye's future. They are so resentful and hopeless that they don't even need to think about Türkiye's future anymore.

Let's listen to Halil Inalcık:

"What a great exuberance echoed throughout the country when Mustafa Kemal Pasha took the podium and enthusiastically started addressing his people for the first time with the starting words "Büyük Türk Milleti - Great Turkish Nation". Now you can't understand retrospectively. Everyone was looking at each other in astonishment. There has not been a single ruler in these lands in the last 700 years, who would start his speech by saying Turk. Imperial edicts would begin with "O my servants, it is my command". The stone, soil and plant of Anatolia were not accustomed to this embrace. It wasn't easy for the masses to get over the surprise address. In particular the "devshirmes" who had been making their living around the palace for centuries, felt themselves put in front of the door. Some of them surrendered and accepted, some of those who did not, took on a religious or an ethnic identity and would embark on a long, stealthy struggle in the newly established state."[104]

Here's what Nietzsche says about the losers:

"Unsuccessful people who can't get what they want scream in anger. "Damn this world". "If I can't get what

---

[104] Halil İnalcık…

I want, no one can get it. Let no one be anything". This disgusting feeling is the height of envy".[105]

Finally... The state now belongs to the people. And if someone says, "This state is not mine", his conscience may well justify betraying it.

Media

Let us use the metaphor of a teen ager for media. A bully tries to force him/her into illegal acts. He/she asks dad for help. Should dad help? Or do nothing about it? With no help, the kid collapses and yields.

We talk of a free press. Is it really free though? At a conference I gave at the Bahçeşehir University, School of Government and Leadership, I said that the press is free in the USA. Yes, it is free and unrestrained in the countryside, anyone can say and write anything in minor papers and TV's. The system does not fear them, and lets them free. Why? No impact. No serious threat to the system.

In fact, this policy lets rural people let off steam, eases tensions while small, and prevents social pressure before it builds up. The same policies aim similar ends with liberal policies for rural street protests in the game of democracy. If not, social heat builds up and intensifies, and especially in economic crises, outbursts explode like

---

[105] Friedrich Nietzsche, Tan Kızıllığı, Çev. Hüseyin Salihoğlu ve Ümit Özdağ İmge Publishing Yay., Istanbul, 2020, p. 91

a blocked pressure cooker. Then the state has to take drastic action to reinstate law and order.

Talking about democracy, how about the major media in the USA and Europe? Well, that's a different story. To become a manager or columnist in the mainstream media in Western nations, one must prove his loyalty to the system through harder trials than the intelligence chiefs of those countries. An author, without proving his loyalty and obedience to the system, and without developing his "auto control" abilities against his noble instincts, cannot ascend to the towering ranks of the system.

The Western main media is conformist, happy, and moves in sync with the conductor's baton. And Turkish main media? Wow. No conductor, random commentators who don't know, nor realise where their words lead to. More sentimental, like many in oriental media, than objective and calculated. Many copy and paste foreign news from international Western news agencies without filtering them through their national glasses, nor questioning the aim or manipulations they intend.

Yet again, like in Western main media, one part of the national media is controlled by an international interest, and obeys the baton of the global orchestra conductor. This is especially so for the media of the Westernised devshirmes of Türkiye. When we say the international orchestra, we mean the cosmopolitan global, transnational capital, its media, so-called nongovernmental organisations, and local business associations they control.

If a State is indifferent to these foreign interests, and behaves like the kavat (pimp) husband, then the press starts going to bed with foreign interests. But if a government starts to protect the freedom of its press from foreign blackmail and pressure, sues Turkish journalists in the service of foreign interests, bang. The orchestra starts. "There is no freedom of the press, there is dictatorship, there is autocracy in Türkiye." Many readers from developing countries shall remember their own countries having the same experiences.

The most serious threat to developing countries is, in the face of conditioning, manipulation, and brainwashing techniques, it is nearly impossible to respond to these accusations. There is only one panacea. An opposition with unwavering diligence against foreign interests, and in full solidarity with the government. And for the government, it is a must to give its people the widest possible democratic field, in cooperation with the opposition. Any antidemocratic measure shall be used by foreign interests, not because they love the Turk, but to use democracy and human rights as a political weapon against the Turk. Without widespread awareness, unity, and cooperation across the country, this critical threat cannot be stopped. People who have not yet reached the level of the Nation State would not realise that a threat to the "state" will hit their very individual interests; that the state is their state. Many a Turkish devshirme don't care anymore.

And now, let's see how juntas made coups in Türkiye. First, remember Atatürk's warning that the capitalists may synchronise their interests with foreign interests. It happened so. As capital accumulated, and some capitalists flourished, they saw the benefits of owning and controlling the media like in Western countries. As they were in the same devshirme league with junta generals, the naïve children of the rural populations, they instigated generals with their sensitive points: "Ataturk is being forgotten. Laicism is being destroyed. Islamist bigots are coming to power". And always the same slogan and always the same slogan. Big business and its media knew it worked flawlessly every time.

Then comes the people's revolution, the Anatolian Revolution. The people seizing power from the devshirme, not to give it back forever. They send junta generals to their barracks not to ever roll their tanks against their own nation.

Their leader, like the able husband, protects their media from foreign agents. And the orchestra starts again: There is no freedom of the press in Türkiye. Translation: The press is not a mistress to Western interests; the West cannot prostitute it anymore. Erdoğan, preventing the Western interests, is an autocrat. To repeat, I think the oppressed peoples of the world reading this book will identify with these lines and bitterly think that the same game is being played in their own countries.

For the Western populace to realise: The developing world is awakening, especially the former colonial peoples. They started to understand the game. Westerners, however, are sound asleep and believe that their press is free and their governments are democratic. They also don't know where they are being led. They will wake up as their economic prosperity declines.

Before wrapping up our chapter, let me share a memory from Chicago. (1994-1998). When we met on various occasions, I used to chat with a well-known journalist in Chicago. At the time, I was interested in the decline of American share in the global economy, and wanted to make a comparison of percentages as of post-WW II and 1990s. As we did not have ChatGPT then, I asked the journalist if he knew the ratio. His reaction, I cannot note here. He treated me like a spy who was trying to engage him. He may have been correct in behaving so; intelligence officers often bait journalists and potential spies by approaching them with innocent questions. It turns out that US intelligence trains or informs its journalists on counter-intelligence techniques and enables them to develop automatic reflexes. I wonder... In which realm is our press and intelligence on these issues?

Identity in the Republic

Ottoman Empire fell, and the devshirme bureaucracy vanished as well! A rational political scientist wouldn't say anything like that. Officers and devshirme bureaucrats educated in Abdulhamid II schools were the founders of the Republic. To repeat, the Republican founders were the unbroken continuation of the Young Turk and Union and Progress movement.

Listen to Çetin Yetkin now:

"As the results of the municipal elections were coming in, Atatürk asked (his personal assistant) Hasan Rıza Soyak which party had won. After he replied "our party", referring to the CHP, Atatürk said, "No, it's not like that at all! I'll tell you which faction won. The winner is the governing party, kid! Actually, they are the gendarmerie, the police, the district manager, the district governor and the governors... Do note this!".[106]

Atatürk's common sense, "How happy is the one who says I am a Turk" was the answer to the "identity" problem occupying the minds of the thinkers of the late Tanzimat period and the early Republic. Just as we respect individual identity when a person says call me by my name, we also respect the social identity of those who say, "I am Turkish". "Turk is the one who says I am a Turk". We should accept those who separate themselves from this identity with respect, too. And acknowledge the identity of whatever a person thinks of himself, whatever social group he sees himself belonging to.

Within specific geographic boundaries, we refer to the broad umbrella at the top of social, political, ethnic, religious, etc. identities. What is Türkiye's dominant identity? Is it embracing enough? Under this umbrella, will sub-identities be able to coexist in harmony and

---

[106] Çetin Yetkin, Karşı Devrim 1945-1950, Kilit Publishing, Istanbul, 2019. p.27

peace with one another? Our hearts yearn for an answer to this question.

A nation sits on a shared past, common lifestyle and common ideals, real or imaginative. If these factors are powerful, inclusive, and in harmony, the nation will be strong, otherwise, it will be weak.

When we look at history for our common past, we see an ethnic structure that is heterogeneous by DNA, but has been harmoniously blended over a millennium. We may formulate it as a synthesis of two dimensions. First would be the "horizontal synthesis", the ethnic mixing of nomads on horseback in the steppes before our entry into Anatolia. Then comes the "vertical synthesis"[107], settling in Anatolia and merging with its indigenous peoples. Except for some of our Kurdish citizens, those who have no problem with this ethnic mix say, "I am Turkish".

---

[107] My vertical/horizontal synthesis idea presented to late poet and intellectual Attilâ İlhan and his inclusion of the idea into his book "Ulusal Kültür Savaşı – National Culture War" Bir Büyükelçinin Düşünce Dünyası, Aydın Nurhan, TASAM Publishing, Istanbul. 2

*"religion is the strongest feature of civilizations, at the heart of both their present and their past."
Fernand Braudel History of Civilisations Pp 22

Our Identity Elements

1. Language

How do we explain our relationship with Central Asia, as our genetic percentage has decreased dearly? We will answer this issue by calling it "Cultural Genetics". The most dominant element of both identity and cultural genetics is language, namely "Turkish". If the person who says "I am a Turk" speaks Turkish, it means that his Turkish identity is strong.

2. Religion

"Islam" is the second component that strengthens Turkish identity. When a Turk professes, "I am a Muslim," his identity is strengthened. As many social scientists including Fernand Braudel* agree, the origins of civilisation are found in religions. They establish a person's civic affiliation.

Ireland is a good example in the narrative. North Irish terrorists during the Catholic-Protestant conflict stopped and asked a passerby, "Are you Catholic or Protestant?" The smart young man could not figure out their identity and replied, "I am an atheist". This time, the terrorists questioned, "Are you a Protestant atheist or a Catholic atheist?" This tale is a good illustration of how someone could be a prisoner of the cultural identity they were born into.

In order to test the power of language and religion in identity, it is a suitable method to look at Turks who marry foreigners abroad. If a child born from marriage to a foreigner does not know Turkish and learns the language of his foreign parent... Likewise, if he takes the religion of the foreign parent, he will assimilate in a single generation and lose his Turkishness. Even if he says "I am Turkish", future generations will have nothing to do with Turkishness. Former British Prime Minister Boris Johnson, the grandson of a Turkish Çankırı Kalfat peasant, is a good example.

Take another dimension. What happens if religion and language begin to wear out at home? Take Africa. Where imperialists have altered identities, "name, language, religion" of millions... Take for example, Japan, Korea, China and India where Christianity spreads like wildfire. And its future effects on Asian identities. A third dimension... Think of Abrahamic religions, glues of many civilisations and nation-states, weaken and give way to deism, agnosticism and atheism.

3. Life Style

"Lifestyle" is the third factor that shapes our identity, along with language and religion. Especially for Americans, "Our Lifestyle" is like a faith, like a religion. They want to spread it to the world with a missionary zeal. Opposition to it is seen as hostility.

Our 90% peasant society's way of life at the start of the Republic was very different from the 93% urban society's lifestyle in 2023. How did the peasant lifestyle evolve into a cosmopolitan, metropolitan lifestyle? What influence does technology have on the unification of global societies? How similar is our way of life to that of the merging global village? Should we completely meld into the global village's lifestyle? How much should we stay as ourselves? How long can we remain unaltered?

Take a pen and make a list. Ask yourself questions like a psychiatrist wants you to ask yourself. Which values would you like to preserve that you think make you a Turk? Which values do you think distinguish you from others? Why would you want to stay Turkish? Do you want to stay Turkish? Questions which would create storms in your brain. Serious questions to be composition subjects in our schools.

National Dream

Behind language, religion, and lifestyle, shared ideals ranks fourth among the factors that define us. Take a community spiritually torn apart, where political hatred and enmity have skyrocketed. What common ideals can they share? If your political opponents do good things for Türkiye, will you deny yourself the joy of your country's success stories? Will you be unable to share that joy due to your political animosity?

A nation without common values cannot have common ideals. Ask yourself. In fifty years, what kind of Türkiye do you want to leave for your grandchildren? How realistic are your dreams? What will you do to realise them? What sacrifices are you ready for the lowest common denominators of your nation? Without blaming others, "But they should also..."? The old values are so thoroughly worn out, that we have a tough job ahead of us in making up our minds for new values, then ideals.

Our lumpens transforming from peasantry to a new bourgeois class will learn to "respect" their compatriots in time, and then will come the common ideals of the Republic. Whether they want it or not, their new culture will be rooted in the colours they get from history, religion and tradition.

Our Kurds

Contentious issue: Is there a Kurdish Question in Türkiye? "There is a Kurdish problem", is the major response. "Perhaps there is a Turkish problem", others say. A wide circulation, a symbolic number, the saying goes as there are 22 ethnicities in Türkiye. Another symbolism is the number of states Turks have founded in history, though much more, set to be 16 as symbolised in the presidential coat of arms.

Our ethnic groups, including perhaps two-thirds of the Kurds, have voluntarily united under the banner of Turkishness since the founding of the Republic. Not just them, either. Many of our non-Muslims converted to Islam and joined the Muslim community, and many of our Alevis became Sunnites in history. Then came the Republic with the assertion of creating a modern, uniform nation. As it tries to format religious and ethnic groups into a single mould, it gets an equal resistance to the impact it made in assimilating them. Conservative, pious Sunni Turks resisting Westernism, Alevi Yörüks and Kurds resisting national mix, were seen as threats to the central bureaucracy for many years, as in Ottoman history.

The issue then becomes: Why did some Kurds refuse to participate or resist, while many of them and 22 other ethnic groups willingly, knowingly, and enthusiastically assimilated into Turkish identity? Let us see what the founding devshirmes of the Republic had in mind as creating a new nation-state from the ashes of the multiethnic Ottoman Empire. Initially, they thought of a new state of Muslims, as a partnership of Turks and Kurds.

Founders presented the Republic as a Turkish-Kurdish joint state after WW I, but later, seeing foreign manipulations to use Kurds against the new state, decided to dissolve the two ethnic groups into one Turkish identity. According to this policy, and its offshoot Lausanne Peace Treaty with Western countries, Türkiye was a Muslim country, and non-Muslims were accepted as the minorities, namely Greeks, Jews and Armenians. This policy was effective in the metropolises until the 1980s (the rhetoric of "I am an İstanbulian, born and raised in Istanbul, I am a Kemalist, I am an Islamist" helped the desire to be under the umbrella of Turkishness). With the acceleration of migration from Eastern cities to the West, the assimilation capacity of the great metropolis collapsed. And when Erdoğan came to power, he acknowledged the rights of Kurds as an ethnic reality of Türkiye. Yet the problem continues. HDP, the representative party of the terrorist group PKK, getting about 10% of the votes, wants to declare Kurds as a minority of Türkiye and tries to dictate special minority privileges which the other 21 ethnicities do not claim.

In reality, what they want is to go back to the Ottoman policies of letting ethnic and religious groups into their own lifestyles, ruled by their own local religious and community leaders. Yet those policies of decentralisation cannot work in a nation-state. As we said, the Ottoman regime was despotic in the sense that the people indeed had full freedom of lifestyle, but never ever let them be involved in politics. Could the feeble Republic, after an exhaustive war, afford such a luxury while building a new nation? Kurdish terror organisation PKK talks of oppression of Kurds. Many a time, devshirme rulers saw pious Muslims as a greater threat than the secularist, communist PKK, and tried to oppress the Islamist lifestyle as a greater threat than Kurdish independence efforts from Türkiye. For many years, Alevi Turkmens too, were seen as a threat to the central authority, a continuation of the historical schism.

Although the periphery, without exception, all ethnic, Sunni and Alevi groups suffered throughout history, including in the early Republic, today, only one part of the Kurdish population makes it an issue and wants to secede from Türkiye. Such a wish cannot be realised without war, and that is what PKK is doing. It may have succeeded if Ottoman decomposition were to continue. They do not realise, they have no chance (no matter how much American and European support they get), they are fighting against a vigorous young Republic on the rise.

Yes, the United Nations estimates may say there may be 250 member states by the year 2050, nation-states may decompose, and it may be possible for Britain, France, Spain, Germany and Italy of feudal origin, but not for for Türkiye on the rise. As Kurds are distributed historically into many countries in the region, they may, like in Northern Iraq, succeed in the long run to form their own nation-state, but not in Türkiye.

Taking this opportunity, we should note that Kurds were banned from speaking Kurdish among themselves (not even a mother to his son when she went to visit him at the prison), no print in Kurdish, no songs to be played in Kurdish. Then came Tayyip Erdogan and recognised the human and democratic rights of these groups. Now, Türkiye has legal Kurdish TV, media and music peacefully enjoyed by all.

Our Turkish Language

We have emphasised above that language is the first element of our identity. It is the glue, medium of communication, sympathy, and mutual comprehension among the nation. Language barrier results in a mentality gap and a breakdown in communication. And it would not be an exaggeration to say that the communication barrier was perhaps the most important factor in the schism between the rulers and the ruled of the Ottoman Empire.

This is why when the ruling Young Turks decided the movement of "Halka Doğru – Embrace the People", they felt compelled to simplify the Ottoman language to communicate with the Turkmen.

As for the Turkish language, hailing from millennia, it is one of the most perfected languages, especially with its mathematical verb system. It is suitable for computers, mathematics and logic, and formats practical intelligence in humans. It helps its users approach life not with a fuzzy mind, but with a fresh, vibrant mind with an easy capacity for adaptation, rather than philosophical sophistication.

While we were nomads on horseback, our main need in action was verbs. Hence, our language was predominantly verb-based. Then came settlement and the need for sophisticated nouns and adjectives. As we filtered from Asian steppes to Asia Minor through Persia, we were heavily influenced by Persian Civilisation, and imported Persian words, and rooted words of the Persian language as well. A millennium later, we see the same similar practical acquisitive spirit in Atatürk translating and adopting European laws in urgent need.

Back to language, words borrowed from Arabic and Persian enriched Seljouk and Ottoman Imperial languages, especially where they were needed. Literature and official correspondence of the state. The point that draws attention here is that although there are complaints that Arabic and Persian terms have invaded our language, powerful Turkish grammar and Turkish verb system have remained as the base, and not succumbed to Arabic and Persian, which are again, among the most powerful languages of the world.

Although Persian and Arabic words also affected the Turkish of the nomad Turkmen, their complex forms could not penetrate the periphery. We can easily understand our great Sufi poet Yunus Emre (contemporary of Rumi) of the 13th century, yet we, the new Turkish generations, cannot read and write the Ottoman elite language, neither can we understand it. It was the language of a great civilisation, like Latin; now it is dead and a field for academic studies.

Interestingly, the Tanzimat "Halka Doğru - Embrace the People" movement and the efforts of lifting the language barrier with the people veered off course in the Republic. With a new reinvigoration in the 1960s, the new fashion of "Pure Turkish" went to levels of mania. Everybody, authority or not, started creating a so-called Turkish-rooted word, scientific or not, to replace an Arabic or Persian origin word.

Trying to get rid of Arabic and Persian words from Turkish, Judges wrote in the new nonsensical creations, a jargon which nobody understood. Legal terms in so-called "Pure Turkish" created confusion and havoc. Devshirme class, the alien elite, could again find a special language to separate themselves from the people.

Students could not understand school books written in the newly created nonsensical Turkish words. Those who studied in high school in the 1960s (like the author of these lines) will, for example, remember "logic" textbooks for high schools, which also caused serious confusion. To sum up, for roughly fifty years, there was a communication gap between the Republican elite and the general public.

Like any fashion, this crazy ideological era eventually lost steam; as things calmed down, the pendulum came to a standstill, and modern Turkish, which we all speak today, settled in. This time, however, communication with the populations of the Turkic Republics of Asia, who still kept Arabic and Persian words in a much milder form than the Ottomans did, was disrupted.

Language of thought. The Ottoman language was indeed a language of thought and great literature, able to borrow words from Arabic and Persian anytime it needed a new concept. It had an ocean of vocabulary of three languages at its service. (Like the American English of our day) Modern, trimmed Turkish has just a percentage of that huge ocean. Hence, frankly speaking, Turkish thinkers of our day are the ones who can think in both Turkish and another rich language of the world. I hope I'm wrong.

Here, I shall dare to accuse TDK, Türk Dil Kurumu – Turkish Linguistics Foundation personally founded by Atatürk, still being funded in millions of liras from his estate. They failed to manage the "Pure Turkish" orgy of the 1960s, in fact, poured gasoline on the fire with their non-scientific, ideological approach.

Today, the greatest problem in the Turkish language is the problem of pronunciation. Because of the transformation from Arabic to Latin alphabet, many Arabic and Persian origin words cannot be written in correct phonemics. TV speakers, TV series artists, Professors and famous politicians, and role models for young generations, all make great blunders in pronunciation. For written grammar, I would challenge all of them (myself too) to write a paragraph without major mistakes. The fact that their errors are not taken seriously demonstrates how poorly we care for the Turkish language, which is our mother tongue. Let's call it shortcomings of the lumpen transition process in education.

This chaos can only be fixed by a reform in education and by creating an atmosphere of love for our mother tongue, ostracising and mocking the role models who make blunders in using our mother tongue.

As for the Turkish Language Foundation TDK, with millions of liras to spend on Atatürk's estate, it can send free experts who can serve as pronunciation coaches on television news stations and TV soap opera sets. They should also send experts to national newspapers. Spelling and grammar mistakes in newspapers are simply unacceptable. There should be no compromise with the editorial profession. Since universities are unsuccessful in educating our elite with adequate ability in our mother tongue, TDK may establish a special institution to train aspiring candidates for journalism and performing arts. A law can be passed imposing the rule, anyone without a certificate from such an institute cannot go on TV or on stage.

Before closing our subject, it is worth noting a folly: modern devshirmes hating Arabic and Persian words are very happy to learn, use and import English words into new Turkish, just as their Young Turk ancestors learned, using and importing French words into the Ottoman language. Fashion of the day. Is it not?

Religion

Where does religion stand between the devshirme and the reaya? Let's look at the name Turkmen:

Prof Ahmet Taşağıl says: *"**Turks who became Muslims, began to be called Turkmen**. It's about the Oghuz... Especially after the 880s, when the Oghuz (root of Turkmen race) started to become Muslims in the Fergana region, East of today's Uzbekistan, the name Turkmen was used for the first time."*[108]

And Prof Göka again: *"Brother quarrel continued after the Turks converted to Islam and arrived in Anatolia. Between Muslim Turks and non-Muslim Turks, and between Seljuks and Turkmens. Schism between Madrassah Islam – Tekke Islam, Official Islam - Folk Islam continued during the period of (Anatolian Turkmen) kingdoms."*[109]

It's interesting to note that the Seljuk and later Ottoman governments who adopted Islam forced Sunni Islam on the Turkmen, and labelled those who disobeyed as infidels. A thousand years later, the Republican regime made a 180-degree turn, and started imposing French laicite on Sunnis, this time labeling the Sunni periphery as bigots. Thus, the Ottoman rupture between the state and the reaya became even more radical in the Republic. In response, the periphery, which is now Sunni, accused the positivist, materialist rulers of the Republic of being unfaithful. In other words, we see the centre and the periphery constantly alienating one another in terms of religion and lifestyle.

---

[108] Ahmet Taşağıl, Türklerin Serüveni Metehan'dan Attila'ya, Fatih'ten Atatürk'e, Ed. Cansu Canan Ülgen, Kronik Book, Istanbul, 2019.
[109] Göka, 2006, ibid. p. 252

Today, as in history, we see a deep gap between the interpretations of religion among the ruling elite and the ruled. Ottomans, trying to assimilate them, forced the Alevi Turkmen to settle down and become Sunnites. Now, Republican elites who chose positivism, and followed the Christian example of Europe interpreted both Sunnism and Alawism as personal psychological choices and "pushed them from the public domain" and "imprisoned them home".

Jean-Paul Roux describes the Turkmen religion as being "unique" and a mix of monotheism and polytheism. In Turks, he says, "folk religion" and "state religion" have always been distinct from one another.[110]

"Those who took control were the Sunnis, and the oppressed and despised, but venerated in wartime by their very kin were the shia Turkmen, the "kara budun - black nation" so to speak. They could manage to keep their own spiritual characteristics in Islam, and keep the ancestral religion alive."[111]

Many Salafist Arabs assert that Turkish Islamic understanding is still under the influence of their pre-Islamic Central Asian beliefs. Villagers in rural Anatolia practice Islam in a much more liberal manner than in Istanbul, where religion becomes uniform and is applied in the mathematical discipline. Then, who can blame the Anatolian rural Turk as a religious fanatic against such a historical background?

---

[110] Göka, 2006, ibid. p. 74
[111] Göka, 2006, ibid. p. 255

There is a saying that goes: "There are as many Islams in the world as there are Muslims." Each person has his own unique idea of god. Every individual has his or her own conception of god and religion.

If we do a little anthropology, who can say that the main issue for peasant women picking crops from sunrise to sunset in the field in sweat and fatigue would be which style should they tie their headscarf?

Could the headscarf—a practice she has been using for thousands of years—be the main issue? The liberal religion that the Turkmen from the Asian steppes brought to the countryside is a peaceful and liberal Islam.

As the village has plenty of time and space, the peasant needs no spiritual, nor physical discipline there. Starting with the town, both space and time begin to be limited and require mental and physical discipline. An example of this in the 1950s was the use of force by officers on the peasant soldiers to impose physical discipline on conscripts in the army. Soldiers had to discipline their bodies, starting with turning left and right.

Then came migration to the city. The city's demand for mental and physical discipline resulted in the standardisation of the turban, or headscarf. A strict interpretation of modernity commanded a standardisation like that of a soldier; there had to be only one standard way of tying the headscarf. The variety of the liberally worn headscarf ties in the village for centuries were no longer permitted in standardised metropolitan Islam.

Political manipulations on such logical turn have no value, just psychological manipulations. The new way of tying the headscarf was an attempt to conform to the absolute logic and discipline requirements of modernity. It's interesting to note that despite its vigorous efforts, the Republic was unable to format and standardise Islamic life and understanding to suit its secular viewpoint. The Turkmen who entered the city, however, was successful in unifying, disciplining and modernising its Islamic lifestyle his own way.

Let's also record Ishak Torun's interpretation of Weber here. *"However, in the process of motivating the world and economic life, religion has also prepared its own end by becoming secular. This is the ironic story of religion (Protestantism) that has emptied itself and driven its soul away from itself."*[112]

As Archimedes jumped out of the bath with his discovery of gravitation, the first to approach religion with a positivist outlook were the early secular engineers of the Republic like the late President Özal and Prime Minister Erbakan. After a severely radical positivist education at Istanbul Technical University, they were the early ones to fall into an identity crisis in search of their spiritual roots. When they read the Quran with their engineer logic, their natural reaction was the literary interpretation of the book which was seen as a radical understanding of Islam by the devshirme rulers of the time.

---

[112] Torun 2003, ibid. p. 114

Engineers waking up to an identity crisis was a new beginning since Tanzimat, a questioning of Westernization, the supremacy of Western Civilisation and laicism. Although intellectually not fully equipped to challenge the Westernised devshirmes, the wake-up trend quickly spread among the newly educated rural. This was not the traditional reaction of illiterate ignorants. The fire of reaction was lit by the best-educated kids of middle-class families. They were challenging the Western clones who were so sure of their supremacy against their "ignorant" peasants who needed to be Westernised by themselves.

A new era was beginning to dawn upon the century-old identity crisis. The Tanzimatist Devshirme Bureaucracy reacted violently to these "traitors" that emerged from within. It was a frontal assault on the secular faith of devshirmes. A group of brilliant engineers from Istanbul Technical University, one of the elite castles, dared to question modernity.

In the beginning, the "Nonconformist Engineers" looked as if they did not have much chance in challenging devshirmes who had the full support of Europe and the USA. But the real issue was deep inside. An issue of identity. Devshirmes have been in an identity crisis for a century. They were bewildered between tradition and Western Civilisation. They had wholehearted faith in modernity. But this faith could not give them the peace of mind between their roots and what they aspired to.

And the other group, the engineers, started to leave their literal interpretation of the Quran and gradually reached a synthesis of their understanding, modernity, and historical Anatolian liberal Islam. The pendulum swinging between matter and spirit came to a harmonious middle way. The trend of urbanisation was; grandmothers wearing a black chador, mothers sporting a coat and headscarf, girls without scarves, and some grandchildren from these families wearing bikinis.

Western transformation may be a good example of Turkish transformation. Take Greco-Roman materialism turning into spiritualism in the Medieval Age, transforming into materialism with Reform, Renaissance and Industrial Revolution, then the age of Postmodernity and fuzzy logic.

Take pre-Islamic Turks, then adopting the spiritual lifestyle of Islam, then the wake-up call of Tanzimat to the materialist world. And the radical swing of the early Republic to secular materialism, a deep rift with the periphery. And 21st century. 93.2% of Urban Muslims approaching the reasonable, middle way. And the religious-laicist quarrel, soothing.

Remembering British philosopher Alfred N. Whitehead saying European philosophical tradition consists of a series of footnotes to Plato, let's say religion tells the philosophers: You go round and round like a grindstone horse with no distance. A human is like a robot with five receptors and a processor. He cannot know beyond its receptor capacity. Likewise, the capacity of the processor is also limited. He cannot know of anything beyond what he can make sense of.

Yet a lovely explanation of philosophy: An enjoyable journey without a destination of disembarkation. And religion answers: I've come to save you from your unanswerable searches. Your brain is in a prison called life, and I've come to set it free so it can experience the freedom of eternity. I am beyond what your five senses and logic can comprehend.

As we said before, there are fashions, including intellectual fashions, and some live for more than a century. For the devshirmes, the intellectual fashion was religion – the culprit which kept the Ottomans behind Europe, and its leader, the Caliph Sultan. To be praised as a modern Western, civilised person, one has to be skeptical, nihilist, or at least keep a distance from religion. Otherwise, the mechanisms of inquisition and excommunication of our Westernist modernists would start working.

Delving into a scientific inquiry, I kindly request your understanding for going into a little privacy. The most striking example of the religion/modernity conflict for the Turkish youth of the 1960s was pubic hair. Turkish cleaning customs include armpit and skirt shaving, both for males and females. Although the tradition was rooted out of religious prerogatives, it turned into more of a Turkish national tradition in historical sequence.

Since the roots of body shaving were based on religion, the youth started abandoning this custom in the 1960s, fearing that they would be considered Islamists by the modernists. Parallel fears were of playing with worry beads and having beards (except ideological and intellectual beards). Anxiety was: "If people at the beach, don't see hair under my armpits... Will they think I'm a peasant, a reactionary Muslim, or bigoted?"

They thought that letting body hair grow was a necessity of civilisation. Leaving hair in the armpit, but not knowing deodorant use.. To rub stool with toilet paper on long back hair instead of using water after toilet. And not have the habit of taking a shower after it... The fears and complexes of a generation that had not yet matured to face the accusations of the Westerners, fueled this unbelievable, nonsensical approach to what was considered civilised behaviour.

Before closing the issue of some of our young people's anxiety about looking modern, let's record another logic game that will make Descartes do somersaults in his grave. Logically, rubbing toilet paper on the back may leave some stool stain on back hair. Now, this is the point of deciding who should enter public pools in France. French authorities assert that hijab is unsafe, against hygiene/health, in pools. So come the homework: A clean body versus a dry-clean body, which is more eligible to enter the pool?

Even these illogical examples will not quench the inferiority complexes of some of our obsessed ones who will support this absurdity.

Let us wrap up the discussion of religion with four quotations from Erol Goka:

"Ones who grasped power were Sunni, whereas the oppressed and despised by the rulers of his own lineage were generally the Shia, just to be remembered in times of war. Yet they were able to add their own spiritual characteristics to Islam, and somehow were able to keep their ancestral religion vibrant."[113]

"According to Çulcu, one of the most important events in Ottoman history was the murder of Çandarlı Halil Pasha of Kalenderi/Ahi origin, with the influence of devshirme pashas. Because this event represents the rapid shift of the Ottoman central administration and state policy towards an Arab/Islamic/Sunni line of bigotry. After this date, the office of Şeyhülislâm, a Byzantine institution, will enter the Ottoman palace. A new tension will begin between the orthodox center and the Turkmen circles, which are close to the heterodox current. As the heterodox authority created by the Safavid state influenced the Turkmen, the central authority's attitude towards them became harsher, but the Janissaries, who shared the same beliefs with the Turkmen, became more and more grumpy."[114]

"In order to centralise and legitimise its power, the ruling clan adopts a belief system (which, like other elements of civilisation, is often borrowed from the surrounding civilised communities) acceptable to all

---

[113] Göka, 2006, ibid. p. 195
[114] Göka, 2006, ibid. p. 233

members of the community. Other tribes creating centrifugal forces, insist on old beliefs and lifestyles and try to resist the center. Thus, a 'national religion' and a 'folk religion' distinction emerged that constantly produced the Mafiosi society structure which would feed continuous fratricidal strife."

"These esoteric movements gained more power during the Crusades and Mongol invasions. On the one hand, there was the "official Sunni madrasah Islam", and on the other hand, "popular piety", influenced by esoteric beliefs and Bâtinism prevalent among the nomadic and peasant elements and in the lower strata of the cities.

The Babai Resurrection of Babas (rural Shia religious leaders), who combined Shamanic and Shiite beliefs with the belief in the Mahdi, emerged on this ground. The distinctions between Madrasa Islam-Tekke Islam, Official Islam-Folk Islam continued in the period of principalities."[115]

"Undoubtedly, there are many other factors in the evolution of the Ottoman Empire towards such a behavior, but it is most likely that they, like other ruling tribes in Turkish history, felt the obligation to choose a foreign religion, lifestyle and management system in order to manage the Turkish communities under their rule, which we have been underlining since the beginning."[116]

---

[115] İshak Torun, Max Weber' de iktisadi Gelişme Düşüncesi, Okumuş Adam Publishig, Istanbul, 2003, p. 109
[116] Göka, 2006, ibid. p. 256

The Need for Dogma

Flashback to the radical materialism of medical students of the 19th century, we can discuss religion as dogma.

How the human brain shall find sound judgement in the freedom of unrestrained and irresponsible functioning is an important issue for Philosophers and theologists. As humans love the freedom of wandering in the endless oceans of thought, they occasionally need a solid, tranquil, all-encompassing harbour to seek refuge in. That port is an absolute, unquestionable dogma. Religions and ideologies both attempt to fill this need. All of them, though, are products of the human brain, so they evolve over time.

At this point, the Qur'an stands out from the others. Non-Muslims assert that the Qur'an was compiled after the Prophet and may have changed, similar to earlier religious texts. Some deists and atheists among our devshirmes also agree with this claim. The claims that the book was changed are only a reference to the period until it was compiled. From the moment the book was compiled, there can be no claim of change because there is only one verse. *"We brought it down, we will protect it (forever)."* (Surah Hicr, Verse 9.) It is a declaration that the Qur'an has not changed for 1500 years and will not change.

Why did we choose this subject? LGBTQ rights are a hot topic right now. Discussions about sex and nudity are as old as humanity itself. Images of police taking measurements of swimsuit lengths on US beaches in the 1930s can be our discussion starter. We can also recall how women dressed in medieval Europe. From pagan homosexuality and nudity in ancient Athens and Rome to medieval covering and then to modern homosexuality and nudity, we observe a cycle. This cycle serves as a reminder that societies, like individuals, can go through rebellious adolescent periods and try to prove themselves.

Through this lens, we can assess the sociopsychological boom times in the areas of women's rights, LGBTQ rights, sex, nudity, etc. Of course, in these discussions, it is important in which periods of history and in which geographies the change took place.

Will Turkish modernity follow the same course as the veiled Europe of the Middle Ages evolved into the Europe of nudist and LGBTQ camps today? What role does this opening play in the claims and aspirations of our people, who seek to leave behind the agrarian lifestyle, elevate themselves to the bourgeoisie, modernise their lives, and demonstrate their freedom? How much will they feel like adults and free once the psychology of rebellion is satisfied?

As the human spirit has been blunted by materialist education and people seeking solace in yoga salons, mental health clinics, and Eastern spiritualist philosophy, does it tell us something that they may be after an unchanging harbour to take refuge in? Could that harbour be religion again?

Law

According to Erol Güngör, *"A nation's laws ought to be officially recognized codes of that community's morality. When laws clash with the ethical norms of a society, people shall be compelled to violate one of the two".*

In the age of the rise, the Ottoman legal system was remarkably just and effective. Providing security and justice to non-Muslims, as well as Muslims, was part of the social contract that the state had with its subjects. Inadequacies and corruption emerged with the decline, especially with the introduction of modernity in the 19th century. It is interesting to note that in the Ottoman provinces, the qadi, provincial judges, were the class that defended the populace from the oppression of the central devshirme bureaucracy. The Republic, ending the duality of center and periphery in jurisdiction, put an end to this protection.

The founders of the new Republic saw that the Ottoman legal system was archaic, bankrupted, ineligible for a modern nation state. Out of desperation, they opted for a hasty translation and implementation of foreign laws. It was against science, yet for them the only option.

But the devshirme class who were to enforce those laws was more important. Direct translation of foreign laws, plus verdicts of judges foreign to the people and its values, were contrary to the realities of Türkiye. This is why Mesut Yılmaz, the late Prime Minister, was saying that you cannot apply EU laws in the Eastern town of Diyarbakır, a very pious city.

And declining self-confidence of devshirme jurists against the threat of rising periphery. The appointment of a CHP lawyer named Yekta Güngör Özden to the Presidency of the Constitutional Court. Next comes CHP Justice Minister Mehmet Moğultay: "I got a Government decree to recruit 5000 judges. Should I have given these cadres to MHP (nationalist party) and RP (religious party) instead of giving them to my party?" An exemplary mentality of the legal level of Türkiye in the 1990s. At that time, the justice mechanism, which had nothing to do with the people and their values, was working perfectly within the homogeneity of the devshirme tradition and there was no reason for CHP to worry about it falling into opposition hands. There are many today who look for those good old days.

Later, FETÖ saw that the courthouse was a much more effective weapon than the military as a means of seizing power, and it really seized it.

When the military courts were closed and the officers were tried by civilian courts, the imprisonment of the officers by the FETO prosecutors was considered a consolation and relief for the oppressed religious people, especially the headscarved ones, who were wailing under pain of the military coups, and led them to look at FETO with sympathy against the military.

Especially those wearing headscarves, despaired of the ultra-laicist justice practices, sought refuge in the mercy of Christian European judges, and became enthusiastic about Türkiye's EU membership. July 15 People's Revolution was also of historical importance for the transformation of Turkish justice. Disconnected from the people and alien to its values, the judges did not suddenly, but gradually, begin to approach the values of the people, to find a balance between justice, the old and the new mentality, and to get rid of the lumpen Kemalist ideology. The CHP could not accept this new situation, and began to declare that the justice that reconciled with the values of the people, was getting away from Kemalist principles and starting to support the AKP. The reality was that people who put the AKP in its service were now putting justice in its service, asking it to approach its values instead of alien values to Anatolian culture.

At this point, we can ask whether judges fear political power. When I completed my law internship in the 1970s, a rumor started to circulate among the interns. A young judge was assigned to the East, where quasi-feudal order was still of relevance. The following day, a local lord knocked on the young judge's door, and placed a gun and a bag of money on the table, telling the young judge to make a choice. The young judge asked for two days to think, and fled the town right away. Naturally, the next question is: Which option would he have chosen if he hadn't managed to flee? If he had surrendered, wouldn't he have been exposed to blackmail throughout his career?

If a person has justice in his soul, he can make just decisions in accordance with reason and conscience, even if he is estranged from the people and their values. That is why the affinity of candidates is not questioned in hiring judges. However, character analysis of a candidate judge is impossible with current personnel techniques. A candidate with a weak character is a lifelong subject to blackmail, which is a significant disadvantage for law.

Literature and Music

Devshirme and the Turkmen were both influenced by the Iranian civilization's widespread impact on the Seljouk and Ottoman Empires. Devshirme by culture, particularly in the literary realm, and Turkmen by Shiism, or religion, in general.

Turkmen's needs for music and poetry were provided by ozan – minstrel who combined poetry and music in their performances – a vibrant and creative art versus royal divan literature, criticised for giving precedence to form, monotony and harmony over the creativity of folk songs and literature.

One possible cause of the banning of Ottoman Classical elite Music following Atatürk's speech at the Turkish Grand National Assembly on November 1, 1934, maybe its historical disconnect from the rural culture.

Then comes urbanisation in the second half of the XXth century. Pop music replaces millennial folk songs and Ottoman classical music. Arabesque trend, depicting the problems of the lumpen underdog in the transition from peasant to urban status, emerges. Jazz, Western pop music, and classical Western music are preferred by the new devshirme elite group.

As contemporary Turkish pop music matures, it will arguably play a crucial role in the unification of the republican devshirme and transforming lumpen. Just as modern Turkish has become our common language of communication, the evolution of a common musical taste will also contribute to our shared identity, perhaps even spreading beyond our borders along with our food culture.

It is important to remember that differences in taste are superficial during times of transformation. There are not yet sharp distinctions between the tastes of the elite and the underdog. Provincial genes do make themselves felt on every occasion. That is why folk and oriental dances are the ending schemes of many high society balls and wedding parties.

Regarding literature: The book. Companion of the lonely man. Verbal culture still predominates in large families, villages, and social neighborhood environments where personal interaction is still vibrant. Hence, there is no time for the book. Not even the concept of it. Then comes the urban apartment and the nuclear family. The lonely person of the metropolis where the neighbor does not know his next-door neighbor. Welcome the friend. The book. Best friend of the lone urban.

In such a process, the book was the best friend in the West for the bourgeoisie. Or for aristocrats who had much leisure time. For Türkiye, the situation is a little different. Before the book culture was firmly established, came the internet.

The internet, together with globalization, and the uniforming effect of technology in the global village, has the effect of merging the tastes of the affluent and the rural. Considering the future of traditional Turkish music, dance, and folklore; we can predict that they will unite the devshirme and the ordinary masses with a uniform taste in the near future.

As for internal orientalism, American military personnel stationed in Ankara in the 1960s created an oriental corner in their homes with rugs, kilim cushions, hookahs, and copper and brass pitchers. The sons of high-ranking bureaucrats, the youth of 1968, used to copy them and create Oriental corners in their homes. A significant psychological topic. Copying Americans, these kids were declaring to the world, "I have risen so high, I have come so far from the village, and now I am very modern." They were shouting, "I use village furniture as decor in my home like a Westerner," without worrying about being branded as a peasant. They had become Orientalists of Edward Said without knowing who they were.

A similar orientalist trend was the interest of college youth in rural folk dances. High society kid felt so supreme, that he was doing folk dances without the fear of being called peasant or backward. Not to forget, in many a field, they still lacked the self-confidence to assert their real roots.

Such was the psychology of many modernizing youth of the 1960s. It may not be an exaggeration if we surmise that future Republican aristocracy may develop from the rising religious class, which would incorporate Ottoman and Anatolian faith and traditional colors into their new lifestyle. No doubt, Western classical music too.

With the emerging urban taste, folk dances, modernized by the "Anatolian Fire" ballet group, may evolve into modern ballet and operas (as Atatürk imagined) and likely become global cultural values.

The music that will eliminate the distinction between devshirme and the people and unite them on a common point is modern Turkish pop music. To note, when you hear French, American, Italian, German, Spanish, Indian, Arab, or even Greek pop music, you will immediately figure out the culture it belongs to. Although it has fans from Turkic world to Arab lands to Athens, we still cannot say that Turkish pop has reached maturity and gained its special modern characteristics, it is still in transformation. Maybe we will have to wait two more generations for it to mature. Until that day, both our devshirme and our lumpen will sing the same refrains.

Regarding how music affects people's souls:

While American music stirs the human spirit and creates a new Turkish generation as a rebellious, combative generation, Ottoman classical music is said to be a music that gives peace and tranquility, hence blamed for numbing the warrior spirit of the Turkmen of Central Asia. Now the question: Numbing music, or combative music? Quarrel or tranquility? Which one would

Ataturk have preferred? The fact is, he always listened to Ottoman classical music. (To note, Sultan Abdulhamid II was a fan of Western opera).

Does America understand that by exporting pop music to other countries, it is fomenting an aggressive global youth? On the one hand, its youth gets aggressive with its music, then on the other, they need dope for tranquility, of no use. A vicious cycle of arousing and numbing effects. And a youth in crisis.

Education

Erol Güngör writes, *"The clash of the education system and socially acceptable moral standards... If, what a person learns at home, is viewed as a fault at school, and what he learns at school is viewed as a crime in court. Then it becomes impossible to know right from wrong and behave morally."*

Characteristics that humans naturally possess from birth and those they pick later from their environment (temporal, spatial, and social) are a serious topic of research among psychologists and philosophers.

As dictionaries define it, education is an attempt to shape and mold human nature. And the issue is, in whose mold shall the kid be shaped? In an age where we discuss the once thought of as futuristic experiments, George Orwell's "1984" and Aldous Huxley's "Brave New World," the most serious question awaiting us is: what shall the education philosophy for the coming age of global cyborgs be? And who shall decide on it?

As we may recall, the original goal of public education after the French Revolution was to create a nation for the state. Training bureaucrats for the state was the earlier goal, as was with the Ottoman elite college Enderun. And the final stage was educating human resources for the economy.

Starting with Enderun, our priority was always educating bureaucrats for the state. Then, the nation. Our people did not make the state. The state made the nation. Especially the founders of the Republic. Economics calls for analytical, logical, and rational minds. Yet our antiquated, archaic copy of French education philosophy tried to produce ideological, irrational, obsessive minds as rulers deemed correct. A mentality which reached its height during the Nazi and Communist eras.

With us, the state ideology was named Kemalism. An ideology that pulled everyone to one side to support his political and world views. An ideology that would have surprised Atatürk if he was to rise from his grave. A peasant ideology based on the memorization of Kuran converted into Atatürk's aphorisms, without any philosophical conceptualisation. Even in universities. Parroting aphorisms by professors, politicians, and so-called intellectuals for a lifetime. Fact! In the 21st century. An ideology that leads to a hell of certificated but unthinking idiots. The aim was not to raise questioning, creative minds, but to raise an obeying uniform peasant population to take orders like North Korea.

In the beginning, the goal of the new nation-state was understandably to unite the remnant Ottoman Muslims coming in from the Balkans, Caucasus and Arab lands in one uniform identity and ideology. Yet the process was unnecessarily extended, corrupted, and even became divisive, nearly leading to the brink of disintegration of the nation. Oppression for uniformity was especially tough on pious Sunnis, alevites and Kurds. What the later devshirmes could not realise was that a suit cut for the peasant society of the 1930s, closed to the world like North Korea of today, was too tight for the 93% urban, open society of 21st century.

An important example: as government imam schools were under the chapter of technical schools of the legislature, the February 28, 1997 military junta, trying to block imam schools, discouraged all technical schools, results of which Turkish industry still suffers. Today, Turkish industry, whose exports are running towards five hundred billion dollars, is like the European post-war industry thirsty for skilled manpower. Rocketing Turkish exports and the industry requiring skilled technical power cannot find enough technicians on the one hand, and unemployment of unskilled university graduates on the other.

As our primary, secondary and high schools, and even our universities, are still trying to raise rote Kemalist mullahs disconnected from real life, Turkish industrialists started opening their own technical training centers, insulated from the indoctrination of outdated official curriculum, focused on industrial production.

And how could the peasant, ignorant junta generals know how they were to ruin the Turkish economy with their archaic ideology of Kemalism? To repeat! Kemalism is an irrational, archaic ideology that is impossible to be imposed on a modern bourgeoisie wide open to the global community of the 21st Century. Above all, it has nothing to do with Atatürk, as claimed.

Further note for those who have seen the modern universities of the Gulf countries will realize with astonishment how far we fall behind the denigrated so-called backward Islamist sheikhs with our dogmatic, ideological, rote curriculum.

Despite the infrastructure that the government has modernized with the best of intentions, our education philosophy is bankrupt and outdated. It cannot even give national consciousness to many of its graduates. And it can no longer be fixed with patchwork repairs.

Let us finish our education chapter by referring to my article dated October 11, 2017.

Revolution in Education: Knowing What You Know Well[117]

Our recently discussed TEOG, or the Transition System from Basic Education to Secondary Education, is

---

[117] Aydın Nurhan, Eğitimde devrim: Bildiğini iyi bilmek, Star Nwespaper Açık Görüş, 11 Ekim 2017. Hiperlink: https://bit.ly/3JGabap

merely a small reflection of our failed educational strategy. Surely, it shall only be a palliative remedy. It is no longer possible to fix education, which is actually bankrupt, out-of-date, and limping even in raising "national" consciousness, with patchwork-style repairs, despite the infrastructure that the government has modernized with the best of intentions.

We need a holistic approach, radical fundamental solutions to our problems. We need a revolution in our education strategy. For 21st century. We have the world's most arrogant, most cocksure education policy of the world.

We claim we can push everything to the student's brain. We end up teaching the least. We rank last among OECD nations. In the age of Google and ChatGPT, we make brains like information garbage cans. We force students to memorize, knowing sure they will forget things within a week.

Let's start with the "education policy". A bourgeois takes five generations to settle. Founding the Republic, we were 90% peasant, 10% literate. Shortly, if my father was the first-generation urbanite, I at 68, am the second, and my kids are third-generation urbanites. Meaning we are still in the process of urbanization and my son's grandchildren shall be real bourgeois. Transforming from a peasant lifestyle to an urban lifestyle is a painful process with chaotic values. Without new values settling, without a national consensus on the new urban values, it would be impossible to reach a consensus on a national education philosophy.

At the present stage, not being ready for a consensus of the devshirmes and ruralites on the philosophy of education, what we can do is leave long-term vision to politicians, and work on the technical aspects of our curriculum. I worked as a high school English teacher. I worked as a lecturer of diplomatic English at the Faculty of Political Sciences of Ankara University. I was astounded and saddened by the lack of English proficiency among senior high school students.

Then our first task should be to take English courses as an example, find out how much the government spends on each student taking English through high school, and then consider what can be done to stop this excessive, pointless, and irrational expenditure.

Digested Information

Let's elaborate on our subject a little more. In our time (in the '60s), there were, I think, seventeen subjects in high school. When the state said that they would put everything into the student's brain, they could not insert anything. The topics that were rushed to be memorized for the exam were forgotten in a few days, and there was no useful, "digested information" for life. What could be the solution? As far as I can remember from what I read in my youth, sports were considered important for body discipline and music for soul discipline in ancient Greece. When we add mathematics, Turkish and history courses to these, five main compulsory courses emerge as the skeleton of our curriculum.

These main, compulsory courses will be taught over and over again every day for twelve years; students will "digest", learn all the subjects one hundred percent. In other words, the Turkish nation will be a nation that knows well what it knows. The Turkish graduate will do his job perfectly. He will do his best, he will be in the spirit of perfectionist discipline, and he will surpass the Swiss perfection. He will not be indolent to save the day. And certainly be a sportsman, doing his best to workout. For body discipline and health. In the age of screen obesity.

Let us now discuss some academic topics. I'm talking about elective subjects. "Enthusiasm" and "Talent" are our two magic words. In addition to the five compulsory courses, students will enroll in as many elective courses as their capacity will allow. Areas in which they are interested and skilled.

Now, when they finish high school and knock on the doors of university, the educators shall see those who have taken only the five compulsory courses due to their laziness. And they will see the successful and eager ones who have taken elective, additional courses.

Here is the caveat. Let's say a kid was good in biology and chemistry courses, the preferred subjects for students planning to pursue a career in medicine. Would it be sufficient to be a medical surgeon? Let us compare a student who has taken carpentry lessons in high school and shown extraordinary dexterity in manual skills. The other student is also successful in chemistry and biology, but inept at physical skills.

Indeed, physical skills shall be deciding factors for the medical field.

In our suggested system, in addition to the five compulsory courses, there can be as many elective courses as the national budget permits. The variation of voluntary subjects can be fifty or one hundred if there is sufficient demand. The state ought to prepare teachers in those fields as long as there is demand. With this system, special students who are gifted or incompetent can benefit from the use of special techniques.

Turkish people are sacrificing when it comes to education.

With devshirme experience in their vein, Turkish parents want to push their kids among the elite of the nation. And they make great sacrifices for their kids. There are families ready to pay twenty to thirty thousand dollars for kindergartens. And we do have the know-how to run these schools. Yet the official archaic ideology ties the hands of competent, innovative private schools in breaking with the mesmerising ideological curriculum into elective courses.

If let free from the outdated shackles, the so-called "Tevhid-i Tedrisat - National Uniformity", these private schools can be centers of excellence. If they were responsible only for teaching the five compulsory lessons as we suggested, the remaining time could be perfectly utilized according to each school's own priority. And children without being racehorses, without getting tired.

Teacher Quality

Now let's come to another technical area. Unfortunately, our teacher quality is very low. Our teachers make very simple pronunciation mistakes. They make very simple grammar mistakes. And these mistakes are also made by university graduates, politicians, even professors, and famous media members. And unaware of their ignorance, they consider themselves elite. We can overcome this problem with technology.

Of the five compulsory subjects, sports and math are the easiest areas. Since these are universal subjects, they can be taught with the most advanced techniques in the world. These lessons can be prepared by the world's best teachers as audio-visual programs, no teachers will be needed anymore. The teacher will be the "instructor", that is, the "moderator" who explains the subjects that are not clearly understood and opens the topic of the day to an exciting, innovative discussion. Actually we already entered this era with ChatGPT and YouTube.

Music is second to sports and math for making use of global technology. Yet, the cultural core of the lessons has to be prepared by local pedagogues.

And the most challenging subjects to adapt to the universal teaching methodology will be Turkish language and history courses because they are the most national areas.

Regarding the objective of education:

As already noted, education has two traditional goals: to produce a uniform nation and bureaucracy. Uniformity of nation is still the aim of the majority of states in the world. That is why education is considered "national education" in many countries. But capitalism forced the national curricula to give priority to producing creative minds for capitalism rather than educating civil servants. Therefore, to stay ahead in global competition, creativity will now be our top priority in education.

Another factor is that literacy is no longer the sole means of learning and communication. The deficiency in school curriculum is compensated for by TV and the internet. The best method of learning is curiosity. One learns something he is curious about. That is what sticks in the mind and gets digested. For example, health, which is of secondary value in school curricula, is one of the most watched programs in morning shows on TV channels.

With advancements in AI, reading will soon be outdated. Now, voice can turn into text, text into voice, newspaper articles can be listened to on the internet, and even these can be translated into foreign languages instantly. In short, the era of boasting of states' literacy rates is coming to an end.

The Speed of Materialism

And finally, the clash of the pious versus the laicist. Take the physical law of gravity and the pendulum. We may agitate the pendulum to extremes, then it gradually comes to a standstill. Human communities also go to extremes when agitated, especially at times of great transformation, then gradually get tired and come to a harmonious tranquility.

In the Middle Ages, education was based on "religion/spiritual". In modernity, religion was found guilty, and education became "material/temporal".

Today, especially in countries that have just woken up to the material goods of this world, materialism has not picked up speed yet, yet it is on the way to rocket.

Kids entering primary school stand on two legs, "matter" and "spirit". In a positivist, materialistic curriculum, primary school students are greeted by teachers who are waiting with axes in their hands. And they start chipping the child's spiritual leg. The more the child reads, the more he loses his spiritual leg. If he makes it to graduation from college, his spiritual leg vanishes, rendering him lame. This materialist one-legged person will turn to yoga studios, psychiatrist offices, and sedatives to treat his future psychological void.

Since our nation is going through a transitional period, waking up to the material goods of this world, and in an orgy of consumption, it is natural for the curriculum to support such a lifestyle. And it would be unrealistic to expect a change in education philosophy before this hunger is quenched.

Since we are not ready for a sound education philosophy today, we may go for a tactical, expert-based focus on areas where we can make technical progress. Remember that it was not Mozart's genius that made him, but his "passion". If we embrace our education philosophy passionately, we can undoubtedly serve our nation well. I was inspired to write these lines by seeing the waste of our country's resources for failed English teaching techniques. A reminder from the days when I was a high school teacher. I hope it will give those who are interested some "food for thought".

Enderun/University

Colleges educating the ruling elite of the USA are called the Ivy League. Graduates of these institutions are like the Ottoman devshirme, ruling over politically unaware masses like Ottoman reaya.

Similar to the Seljuks, the Ottomans needed a special institution to educate bureaucrats for the Empire. In 1363, Murad I established Enderun. With the conquest of Istanbul, the college was transferred to the new capital. The educational philosophy of the school, which is reflected to the present day and still continues, was to alienate the child from the culture and lifestyle of his family.

Not to forget, the Republic is a natural extension of the Ottoman Empire. Bureaucracy, which serves as the cornerstone of the government, is again a direct continuation of the Ottoman bureaucracy. If this is the case, the education of Republican civil servants will be based on the historical philosophy of alienating peasant kids from their roots. In such line, a few universities in Ankara and Istanbul took over the task of producing civil servants for the new state.

Just as we attribute the end of the devshirme class to 15 July 2016, we attribute the end of the devshirme education philosophy to the spread of universities into Anatolia. It is so natural for old professors to oppose provincial universities with various excuses, such as declining quality. You can easily assimilate a kid in an İstanbul or Ankara elite school and alienate him from his rural roots. But when you take the university to the town of the child, you no longer have the chance to assimilate or alienate the kid.

Yes, it is difficult to get into elite devshirme schools. They attract the brightest, true. But then it is individual ambition and soullessness. Provincial schools, on the other hand, are schools that maintain the Anatolian spirit. These schools, with their passionate children, and conscious and ambitious philanthropic businessmen, will soon be able to compete with elite schools, and the most successful local colleges will become centers of excellence in their preferred expertise.

Foreign Affairs

Turkish Ministry of Foreign Affairs is the last bastion of the Ottoman Empire. It is the stronghold of conservative professionalism. Perhaps things should be this way to maintain the state's continuity. Should Turkish foreign policy be revolutionized, or should it be left to evolve? In the age of the speed of light, do we have the luxury of evolution?

What is the essence of the Turkish Foreign Service?

Should our Ministry of Foreign Affairs be the defensive, reactive, game-braking institution of the waning Ottoman Empire, or should it be the offensive, proactive game-maker and risk-taking actor of the rising Republic?

Another question: Should it represent the interests of the people, or the interests of the state as it did for the Ottoman Empire?

How much has it absorbed the culture of the society it belongs to? Should a diplomat perform with a nationalist passion, or should he take a technical, sterile approach? Being non-emotional is an important rule of diplomacy. How much sterility and how much emotion?

The Ministry of Foreign Affairs has been the stronghold of Westernism since Tanzimat to the present. The deep roots of its Westernism can best be seen in the articles and comments of retired ambassadors on international issues. They take anti-West policies of politicians with skepticism and caution, assuming that Westerners still have the historical instincts and power to harm Türkiye. President Erdoğan, representative of the rising Anatolian bourgeoisie, has discarded the late Ottoman defensive diplomacy and launched an aggressive and risk-taking diplomatic initiative for the rising Republic. From the reactions of some of our conservative retired ambassadors, this risk-taking initiative is viewed as hasty and dangerous. This concern is understandable.

There are also signs that support suspicions regarding the clash of diplomats' views with the offensive, risk-taking policies of politicians. The formation of a parallel diplomacy desk within the Presidency and the rise in non-career ambassador appointments are two signs of discord.

Another issue is diplomatic organization, whether it should be based on specialization and desk system on the one side, and generalized, holistic diplomatic practice, on the other. Turkish tradition is for the generalized, holistic outlook on world affairs, using diplomats in incongruent geographies. Given its interests extending from the Turkic world from China to the Islamic world and former Ottoman geography, it is natural for the Turkish diplomat to view the world holistically.

Now the question is: Should Turkish diplomacy keep its historical, imperial, holistic approach to the world? Or should it choose specialisation and desk systems like two other modern empires, USA and Russia?

Perhaps the correct question should be: Are specialization to depth versus holistic generalization mutually exclusive and incompatible methods for diplomacy?

Years ago, when I was the head of the Center for Strategic Research (SAM) of the Turkish Foreign Ministry, I proposed a middle ground. Due to the frequent rotation of diplomats, institutional memory could not be sustained in the Ministry. The same deficiency was relevant for Defense and Internal Affairs Ministries. Today, vital crypto evaluation sent by an ambassador to the center is archived and forgotten when diplomats who read it go abroad on another mission. In order to prevent this handicap, I proposed a cell system in which SAM would keep permanent professionals at the headquarters. I think a similar structure to this system was carried out at the Presidency.

As our Ministry of Foreign Affairs does not have a desk and expertise system, we still do not have specialist experts in vital areas. We have deficiencies in Greek, Arabic, Russian, Persian and Chinese languages. To overcome these deficiencies, we can think of establishing an Academy at the Ministry of Foreign Affairs in cooperation with a university in Ankara. Such an institution can establish a master's program in cooperation with the academic community, and even train foreign diplomats like the Russians are doing. Years back, as I visited the Russian Foreign Ministry institution in Moscow, I was told that they were teaching forty foreign languages (if my memory is correct) to their diplomats, as well as to guest diplomats from friendly countries.

To sum up, the Ministry of Foreign Affairs is experiencing problems with its current staff shortage, insufficient office space and historical structure, and not in a position to synchronize with the speed of Recep Tayyip Erdogan's foreign policy. Time will tell how the transformation will evolve.

Business

Since there was no aristocracy to serve as an example for them, provincial notables and entrepreneurs of the early Republic looked at Westernized and modernized devshirme bureaucrats. Cooperation with bureaucracy was also good for their commercial interests. And in time, the organic bond between today's Istanbul's big capital, military-civilian high bureaucracy and their natural representative CHP was established. And in Republican history, we saw the most striking examples of this organic bond in the collaboration of Istanbul business, its media power, and junta generals in military coups.

Let us also touch upon the external links of this collaboration. When I was the Consul General of Türkiye in Bregenz, Austria, I had hosted the Mayor of Kayseri, Mehmet Özhaseki (Now a Minister), who came to buy cable cars for Mount Erciyes. During our conversation, I remember saying to him, "The grocer accumulating a little capital in the village goes to the town, the merchant who blooms in town moves to the city, the businessman who grows up in the city goes to the metropolis, and the big businessman who grows up there opens to global commerce. We may surmise, a business to go abroad may have a volume of 500,000 dollars as a beginning capital.

Once capital becomes globalized, it parts ways with the government, which has helped it flourish, and goes into the hierarchy of the international business community. The purpose of this anecdote is that, as Atatürk warned, some politicians, juntas and businesses may synch their interests with those of foreign interests.

Especially once growing to transnational size, companies start becoming cosmopolitan, and their commercial interests start overwhelming their national loyalty. And just like the presstitutes we talked about, some businesses may go against the interests of their own nation.

We saw grave examples of it on 28 February 1997, 15 July 2016 and other coups. That is what we have to be alert about.

Here is an intelligence issue: when national intelligence services collect vital industrial and economic intelligence, they have to give it to their industrialists and merchants to compete with foreigners. Which companies? How to maintain justice in distribution?

One last point: Ottoman devshirme, especially the ulema-clergy class, have historical fame for their "İstemezük – A certain NO for any novelty." It was against creativity and change, fearing that it would harm stability and predictability. Despite all their Westernist rhetoric, the Republican devshirmes, by saying NO to every investment for the country, are proving that they indeed are the successors of Ottoman devshirmes.

Interestingly though, is Istanbul's big capital's dilemma. Historically, they are in bed with CHP who are against change and creativity. And it is illogical for capital to be against innovation and investment. Time will tell how they will solve the issue. Logic says they will lock interests with the emerging Anatolian business.

Corporatism

Corporatism is a tool of fascism. Through the establishment of professional organizations and chambers, the fascist state maintains control over professional and business groups. The corporatist project is a very fascinating area of research for our nation. Yes, the state wanted and founded the professional chambers and associations to control business and professional chambers.

When democracy came, they continued functioning. One thinks that they would be against the devshirmes. Yet we should remember that business and the educated were traditionally in bed with devshirme bureaucracy. So when people's rule came, they stayed with the devshirme interests. And against the governments that represented the periphery. It is only natural that today's professional chambers, who got their start on the basis of this stance, are pro-CHP.

And Finally Atatürk

Legitimacy is the first concept that comes to mind when the state is mentioned.

When we consider where legitimacy comes from, the Pharaoh declares, "I am God," and his legitimacy is within himself. With ancient Turks, legitimacy was given by Gök Tengri – Sky God, to Turkish kagans. After Islam, sultans declared themselves to be God's shadows on earth. Then we see the age of charismatic leaders with legitimacy again, in themselves.

The point where global civilisation is, legitimacy is given only by the people.

Conversely, totalitarian devshirme, like his Ottoman forebears, continues to undervalue and oppose the populace. He views the populace as being ignorant, bigoted, and reactionary, and does not believe in receiving their democratic approval.

What should the putschist junta members of the Republic (still subconsciously in janissary spirit) do in this picture? The sultan received his legitimacy from God. They do not believe in getting legitimacy from the "ignorant" masses. Then how do we base their legitimacy? ATATÜRK. Since the putschist peasant generals did not yet know what democracy was, like sultans getting legitimacy from God, they continued to base their legitimacy on a deity, this time Atatürk. And not on the people, and thus continued the Ottoman "shadow game", which they allegedly said they were against. And the Western world… As the putschists were laicist and Westernist, the West had to support them against ignorant, regressive Turks.

See what Psychiatrist Kaan Arslanoğlu says about leadership in Freud's totem and taboo pattern:

"Leader worship is an inherited habit from the tribal order. The leader is God's spokesman, practitioner, even himself. All positive qualities belong to him, all beauty comes from him. The human need to find and worship a leader is almost instinctive. With the increase in intelligence and education level, this need decreases somewhat, but the majority still feels the need for worship. In oppressive systems, leaders become more prominent and worship increases. The situation is both the result and the cause of the feeling of obedience to authority. People want an authority, and when they find it, they start worshiping it. The leader is imitated in every way. The reasoning method of the leader becomes the reasoning method of the society or the group. If the leader is liberal, everyone becomes liberal, if the leader is paranoid, everyone gets paranoid. Even the mimics and gestures of the leader get imitated, thousands of, millions of cartoons of the leader are produced. People identify with the leader, qualities and power they lack, they find in the leader feeling them in themselves".[118]

A fitting description of the putschist: He uses Atatürk as his source of legitimacy. He even imitates Atatürk in his dress. He terrorizes people by using Atatürk as a stick against the people. "Law of Protection of Atatürk" is made for this purpose. Today, if an innocent, eight-year-old primary school student says something against Atatürk, not only him, but his whole family, and his

---

[118] Kaan Arslanoğlu, Politik Psikiyatri/Yanılmanın Gerçekliği, İthaki Publishing, 2005, p.85

teacher shall pay for the offence! A fact. In the 21st century. A lifetime of trauma and terror will be inflicted upon the innocent child. Atatürk's vision of a free society with free thought, a free conscience, and free knowledge cannot be realized under such a terror regime. A brain that has been shaped by repetition and fear cannot be free and creative, read critical philosophy, or expand its horizons. Above all, this pedagogy is what makes the shortage of great thinkers in the Republic.

And the deeper effect of distorting Atatürk is that he is used for opiating the Turkish nation. Marx says religion is opium. Our devshirmes use Atatürk as a faith and opium to stupefy people.

Nietzsche notes that communities, in time, attribute divinity to their ancestors who have protected them from monsters and threats. He even extends the origins of the gods to the idea of their rescuing society from its fears, highlighting their debt to the gods and ancestors that their society would never be able to pay their debts to them.

Same with devshirmes. In the subconscious of the devshirme, Kemalism is not a matter of logic. It is a matter of faith. It is a spiritual, unquestionable gospel of faith. Anyone who dares question it is excommunicated by the devshirmes and informed to the police for a criminal suit. Joke? Real. 21st Century reality of Türkiye. And what does Atatürk want? No dogmas.

Let's go in this vein. Some claim that while the Qur'an is an outdated text written 1400 years ago, and cannot be applied today, they excommunicate anyone who would make similar assertions against Atatürk's 100-year-old words. For them, Atatürk's words and deeds are eternal, and cannot be questioned or altered. Let's remember, the 28 February junta also had a truth, and their ideology was to last for a thousand years. No joke. And the Western democracies bolster these autocrats with full support and encouragement against their "ignorant" people.

Whether viewed positively or negatively, Atatürk is the reality of Türkiye. Even though it has been almost a century since his death, he is still Türkiye's agenda. Why is this so? This question is difficult to answer. There is almost no individual psychological and socio-psychological (Freudian, etc.) historical, objective academic research on the fanatical love/hate of Atatürk in Turkish society. Because Atatürk is not history yet, he is a living element of Turkish politics.

No research has yet been conducted on Atatürk's deification using sterile, scientific techniques. Our academics do not dare to enter this field yet. In reality, this fear is unfounded because the subject is not Atatürk. The issue is why, how and for what purposes he was made a center of faith by devshirmes who are still not aware of the fact that Atatürk was the very person who pulled their rope by deposing their head, the sultan.

No psychiatrist has yet studied the behavior of millions on why they put not one, not five, but ten Atatürk pictures in their homes and workplaces. Or why they put Atatürk's signature on all the windows of their cars. The issue is not Atatürk, but with the psychological and political needs he was deified. As we said above, the first reason is that the peasant juntas, who do not yet know what democracy is, show him as a source of legitimacy.

As for Atatürk's belief, I think a person's most sincere feelings are seen in the death of his mother. The following lines in this son's article with the phrase "Allah" on the death of his mother seem sincere:

Chief Adjutant Salih Bey had reported the death of Zübeyde hanım by telegram.

He immediately replied:

"I am very saddened by the sorrowful news you gave me. Have the deceased be put to rest in the appropriate ceremony. May Allah grant life and peace to the nation."[119]

As for the love/hate approach to Atatürk, religion, when personal, is a matter of faith, yet for statesmen, it is a political, strategic tool. In that respect, Atatürk's faith is beyond our subject, only he and Allah can know it. It is up to us to pray for his soul.

Let's wake up to reality. The peasant society of the 1940s is left behind in the depths of history. 21st Century Türkiye is ninety-three percent urban. Atatürk's use as a source of political legitimacy in Türkiye has expired. The

---

[119] Hasan Rıza Soyak, Atatürk'den Hatıralar, Yapı Kredi Publishing, Istanbul, 2022, Volume 1, p. 6

one who will rule Türkiye now has only one chance: to seek the source of legitimacy in the people and the values of Anatolia. As long as we insist on basing political legitimacy on Atatürk, we will not be able to pass to democracy!

Atatürk's Populist Discourses

Now, in order to understand Atatürk correctly, let's record some of his views:

"For hundreds of years, the Turkish Empire was a complex mass of people with the Turks in the minority. We had other so-called minorities, and their management was the source of most of our troubles. The old idea of conquest. And its minorities. One reason for Türkiye's decline was that it had exhausted itself over this exceedingly difficult question of governance." 13 July 1923

"The youth of our generation was dominated by Ottomanism's indoctrination and influence. Non-Turkish elements of the Empire were given special importance over Turks, the real owners and founders of the state. With a wrong understanding of religion, Arabs were called "kavm-i necib – noble race". Albanians occupying important places in the palace, the military and administration had a special praise. And the Turks were viewed as unimportant secondary masses in the background." 1931

We see conquests and magnificent movements in Ottoman history. This is the strategy of conquest and ruling the entire planet. Yet these conquests and magnificent movements never gave the Turks, founders of the state and realizers of these conquests what they wished, nor served their interests." 22 January 1923

"Yes, we had vast borders and a magnificient empire within those borders. However, the vast majority of people living within that boundless space were never in praise of the essential component, Turk. Or perhaps against them. The small group of Turks had to disperse over wide realms and use force to protect the borders and these peoples. 22 January 1923

"Friends, those who have ruined this country and this nation for centuries are long dead. All youth must believe in it. We shall never let them (devshirmes) return unless our heads are gone, until our blood is shed." September 19, 1924

"This army belonged to the sultan, served his will, and got orders only from him. This army had to yell, "Long live my Sultan" three times a day. We built our new army on entirely new ideas and principles. Our new army is built from among our hardworking peasants, and members of the former army who were dedicated to the defense of the motherland and the cause of our people. Establishing our new army, we had only one objective in mind. And that was, this army would be the army of the people, not sultan's army, representing the interests of the entire people, not just of specific individuals." 4, January 1922

How else can it be expressed that Atatürk was on the side of the Turkmen against the sultan and the devshirme?

The conclusion we have reached about Mustafa Kemal Atatürk is that he desired to awaken those who had spent a thousand years living for the afterlife to this temporal world and make them "citizens." He had a sincere desire for it. He aimed for a shocking, extreme effect. He appears to have discovered what is reasonable, given the dire conditions of his time. Unfortunately, due to the lack of social and economic infrastructure, he was unable to turn the countryside of the 1930s positivist. As we mentioned above, it took a century for his dreams to come true, thanks to the socioeconomic revolutions of Presidents Ozal and Erdogan.

ADVICE TO YOUTH

Dear young friends,

"Don't fear" begins our national anthem.

The greatest obstacle on your path: FEAR OF DAMNATION! EXCOMMUNICATION!

On the path of forming your personality, you will be eager to be accepted into the community of your modernist peers. And look for their sensitivities, which may trigger their reprehensions that you are provincial, bigoted, and regressive. And the champions of such condescending behavior shall be the nearest ones to their peasant roots. Yelling in a crowd, I am modern! Imploring I am not a peasant anymore! Accept me into your modern group. Beyond fearing excommunication, they may be in an effort to forget the historical oppression of their ancestors. This behavior also triggers exhibitionism. Do not aspire to be one of those who try modern life's most despicable behaviors to be praised among the lumpens. Trust yourself. Trust your millennial common sense.

Do not fear the settled, genuine bourgeois. He is the Istanbul Gentleman who has "internalized respect for the human being" and has nothing to do with the peasant or the lumpen in transformation. Perhaps even looks at them with a neutral, if not compassionate, nostalgia.

During the process of building your character, you want to be respected, liked, and accepted by the society. You worry about being shunned and banished. These are typical human reflexes, as we discussed in our chapter on psychology. These are not problems to be ashamed of; they are phases that will pass as your personality matures.

The issue is whether this defect continues into a lifelong phobia into a pathology. And it is a serious threat to our nation. With the fear of being left behind, we observe the urge to hold on to lumpen values out of a conscious and willing desire to leave rural values and join the devshirme. The purpose of this book is to overcome this fear and inferiority complex, and to end the artificial political hatred that arises from this disease.

We are the youth of 1968. While we were students at Ankara University in 1968, combat fatigue and boot were the fashion among our socialists. And in the outer pocket was the Cumhuriyet newspaper. And the college youth proudly boasted in all sincerity: "I am the child of a proletariat!", "I am the child of a doorman!" They sincerely thought they were on the side of the oppressed.

Yes, they wanted to finish college and be shepherds to their people. But they did not realize that they came from their villages to the capital city to join devshirmes, that they would become quickly swallowed, assimilated and estranged from their roots. At the time, those college students were not aware of the transformation they were getting into. That is why many of them are the grey-haired members of the high society of Istanbul today.

Compradors of Western culture and capital, in the words of the late poet and thinker Attilâ İlhan.

And the fashion for Gen Alpha kids? Brand names. To seek non-existent aristocratic pasha roots. To boast of wealth. Can you break out of this new vanity? Can you catch the real spirit of the slogans "I am the child of a proletariat!", "I am the child of a doorman!" and remember your roots?

Can't you invent a new intellectual fashion for an audacious new generation that isn't afraid to question Western ideas, has the courage to stop using Atatürk as a crutch, and is not scared of being ostracised by the lumpen high society?

You shall prove your democratic maturity once you have this civilian courage.

CONCLUSION

The central theme of this book was intended to be the examination of the inferiority complex of a generation that results from transformation and rootlessness. For Turks, there is no absurdity as nobility, as Sultan Mehmet the Conqueror had eradicated aristocracy long before. But the Turk has his "töre", the millennial convention – a convention rooted in tradition and religion, distilled and practiced for more than a thousand years.

Our aim is to question the fate of a generation out of the village, in denial of the values he has left behind, in denial of his millennial common sense, for the sake of appearing modern and contemporary. And in search of nobility.

And in the frontline, "lifestyle". It is a global phenomenon, an upheaval. We are in an era in which all values are in an earthquake. We swing back and forth between being unique and cosmopolitan. The youth is nihilistic and unconcerned with their social identity. They are not even in the initial phase of an identity crisis. They are not even aware of the dangers of the age and environment they have been born into.

Devshirme was the possessor of the state. If the state is no longer his, let it sink. The historical hatred goes: Instead of the Turkish army under General Enver saving Edirne, let the Bulgarian army beat ours. Hatred and jealousy are still continuing. One should no longer expect patriotism from the devshirme. The state now belongs to the reaya Turkmen.

In the colloquial lumpen tongue, the lover says to his girlfriend, you are either mine or of the grave. Last warning to devshirme! If your country sinks, you will, too. Also, the aspiring lumpens in your footsteps. At least care for them.

Surprise

I am also a devshirme. My grandfather is a police officer, my father is an air force officer, I am a diplomat. In the American era following World War II, in the 1950s, I was one of those kids running around in air force garrisons as their parents danced at weekend balls. I am a devshirme who entered American boarding schools at the age of eleven and spent eight years there, then became a diplomat and traveled the world, served in five continents but did not know my home, Anatolia.

My lifestyle is the lifestyle of the devshirme. There is no mistake in similes; if excused, my approach to my people brings to my mind the example of the good-hearted son of the bad king in fairy tales. My father's admonishment to *"always be on the side of the oppressed"* drew me to side with the Anatolian people, even if I'm not one of them. I tried to understand the system that oppressed them for centuries. As a civil servant, I tried to do my best to protect my countrymen against injustices. This book was born from those efforts.

I'm not a commoner though. I am a devshirme from Çankırı. And beyond sentimentality, ideologically, as a statesman, I am in favor of the devshirme system. Let's not forget that even the great thinker Nietzsche wanted the best (übermensch) in the world to dominate, and the others to be dominated by them.

In the 21st century, Western prosperity will collapse and this will be the age of democracies to degenerate and pass into autocracy. The lobbying system of the US Congress gives signals of possible corruption and collapse. Salvation is in the Platonic aristocracy (although Nietzche opposes hierarchies) and the Presidential System. The summary of my entire book is that there should not be a rupture between the values of the ruler and those of the people he rules; there should be no gap, alienation, or hatred among them.

Am I a traitor to my class?

If whom we are talking about are the corrupt tyrants who have oppressed my ancestors in the provinces, looked down upon them, and continued such behavior in the Republic, especially since the 17th century, I am not of them. To be fair, in our rising Republic, we also have politicians, intellectuals, and bureaucrats who are willing to support the oppressed. Together, we can create a system that treats our people with kindness, mercy, and compassion. It's not impossible. In fact, I yearned to be what Psychiatrist Erol Goka complimented with the title "organic intellectual of the nation." I'm not sure if I deserved it.

I've addressed the opposition to devshirme in this book from the very beginning. I dealt with the devshirme's alienation from the people. I talked of the people's revolution that got devshirme bureaucrat rule down.

But, the best system fit for Turks is the very devshirme system. Stability requires a presidential system and devshirmes. One caveat is that the modern devshirme will share people's values, will not alienate from them, and the people will be in constant control over them. In this regard, it is crucial that the universities expand to the provinces. After acquiring a strong sense of identity, our universities may start giving their best academics to a national modern Enderun, like Harvard or ENA of France.

Finally, in this book, I touched on human psychology, aspirations, and inferiority complexes. In a sense, it is like the psychological warfare technique. I talked about the desire to be admired, the fear of being excommunicated, and conformism. I tried to "shake the faith" of our modernists a bit in a Socratic fashion.

I had been doing this for years, I was already excommunicated from the school and professional environment I belonged to. I'm not the only one who's been excommunicated from his class. Many of our intellectuals and academics who produced sincere thoughts for their country, especially İdris Kucukomer, were excommunicated in this country.

The great reward of excommunication is Nietzsche's "Loneliness". And the gift of loneliness is "Infinite Freedom". Now, I am ready for much more severe reactions than before, from those who shall read my book, and worse, reactions upon hearsay without reading it.

Modern major media moguls of the Western world are begging to hear the reactions of their readers, including the most hateful. Why? Because the reader's reaction is a fortune that widens the horizon of the author and opens new worlds for him. Response, including the worst, pays off to the author.

But what does the reader gain?

Until it is written down, a thought belongs to its creator. Anything that is written down becomes public knowledge. It is the reader's responsibility to quarrel with the idea, not the author. It is necessary to read an idea objectively, with empathy, and in an effort to comprehend its true intention before deciding whether to support or oppose it. Those who are able to do this will gain as much as the author gains from writing, leave their reading session and gain new horizons. Let's hope they did.

RESOURCES

The following works that I refer to in this book are the books that I thoroughly read and annotated, but then forgot.

It has been said that the reader becomes the heir of the intellectual accumulation of the author he reads.

I wonder if I was inspired by the authors I read and brought their thoughts from my subconscious?

A.C.S. Peacock
Büyük Selçuklu İmparatorluğu
A. Afetinan
M. Kemal Atatürk'den Yazdıklarım
Abraham H. Maslow - A Theory of Human Motivation
Ahmet Arslan
Felsefeye Giriş
Ahmet Cihan
Osmanlı Toplum Yapısı ve Sivil Toplum
Ahmet Davutoğlu
Stratejik Derinlik
Ahmet Önal, Erhan Afyoncu
Osmanlı İmparatorluğunda Askerî Darbeler ve İsyanlar
Ahmet Taşağıl
Türklerin Serüveni, Kök Tengrinin Çocukları
Ahmed Rashid
The Resurgence of Central Asia, Islam or Nationalism
Alain de Botton
Statü endişesi
Albert Hourani

A History of the Arab Peoples
Aldous Huxley
Brave New World
Ali Akar
Türk Dili Tarihi
Ali Arslan
The Turkish Power Elite
Ali Tayyar Önder
Türkiye'nin Etnik Yapısı
Alev Alatlı
Şimdi Değilse Ne Zaman?
Andrew Mango
Atatürk
Andrew Wheatcroft
The Ottomans
Aristoteles
Politika
Arnold Toynbee
A Study of History
Attilâ İlhan
Ulusal Kültür Savaşı
Auguste Bailly
Bizans İmparatorluğu Tarihi
Aziz Nesin
Ah Biz Ödlek Aydınlar
Bernard Lewis
What Went Wrong, The Middle East, 145
Bozkurt Güvenç
Türk Kimliği
Bozkurt Güvenç, Gencay Şaylan, İlhan Tekeli, Şerafettin Turan
Türk İslâm Sentezi

Carl Gustav JUNG
Psikoloji ve Din - Dört Arketip
Celal Yeşilçayır
Thomas Hobbes'un Geleneksel Siyaset Felsefesine Karşı Çıkışı
Cemal Kafadar
Between Two Worlds
Cemil Meriç
Bu Ülke
Cengiz Aytmatov
Gün Olur Asra Bedel - Cengiz Han'a Küsen Bulut
Çağlar Solak
Sosyal Dışlanma Olgusunun Koalisyonel Psikoloji Bağlamında İncelenmesi
Çağlar Solak, Mert Teközel
Sosyal Dışlanma Olgusu Üzerine Genel Bir İnceleme
Çetin Yetkin
Karşı Devrim 1945 – 1950
David Mc Dowall
A Modern History of the Kurds
Dilek Takımcı İmançer
Sosyal Psikolojik Açıdan Stereotip Kavramının Dil ve Metin Analizinde Kullanımı
Dimitri Kitsikis
Türk Yunan İmparatorluğu
Edhem Eldem
Osmanlı Kenti Halep İzmir İstanbul
Erhan Afyoncu, Ahmet Önal, Uğur Demir
Askerî İsyanlar ve Darbeler
Edward Gibbon
The Decline and Fall of the Roman Empire

Edward Said
Orientalism
Eflatun
Devlet
Erik Zürcher
Orta Asya ve İslâm Dünyasında Kimlik Politikaları - Bir Ulusun İnşası, Jön Türk Mirası
Erol Goka
Türk Grup Davranışı - Cumhuriyet Kimliğinin Sosyopsikolojisi - Türklerin Psikolojisi - Türk'ün Göçebe Ruhu - Yedi Düvele Karşı Türklerde Liderlik ve Fanatizm
Erol Güngör
Ahlâk Psikolojisi ve Sosyal Ahlâk, Kültür Değişmesi ve Milliyetçilik
Felipe Fernandez Armesto
Millenium - A History of the Last Thousand Years – Civilisations - Culture, Ambition, and the Transformation of Nature
Fernand Braudel
A History of Civilisations
François Georgeon, Paul Dumont
Osmanlı İmparatorluğu'nda Yaşamak
Fuad Köprülü
Türk Edebiyatı Tarihi, Origins of the Ottoman Empire
Fulya Ereker
Dış Politika ve Kimlik:İnşacı Perspektiften Türk Dış Politikasının Analizi
Francis Fukuyama
The End of History and the Last Man
Friedrich Nietzsche
On the Genealogy of Morality, Ahlâkın Soykütüğü
George Orwell - "1984"

Giles Milton - Paradise Lost
Gisela Eife
The Development of Alfred Adler's Individual Psychology, - Theory of Personality - Psychopathology - Psychotherapy (1912-1937)
Gül Akyılmaz
Osmanlı Devletinde Yönetici Sınıf Reâyâ Ayrımı
Gustave Le Bon
The Crowd: A Study of the Popular Mind
Haldun Gülalp
Laiklik, Vatandaşlık, Demokrasi
Halil İnalcık
Köy, Köylü ve İmparatorluk - Turkey and Europe in History - Economic and Social History of the Ottoman Empire 1300 1914 – Şair ve Patron - Osmanlılar, Fütuhat, İmparatorluk, Avrupa ile İlişkiler - Atatürk ve Demokratik Türkiye, Osmanlılar
Halil İnalcık ve Mehmet Seyitdanlıoğlu
Tanzimat
Hasan Basri Karadeniz
Osmanlılar ile Anadolu Beylikleri Arasında Psikolojik Mücadele
Hasan Cemal
Kürtler
Hilmi Yavuz
Alafrangalığın Tarihi
Hüseyin Rahmi Gürpınar
Şıpsevdi
Ian Morris - Why the West Rules—For Now
Ibn Khaldun
The Muqaddimah An Introduction to History (Edited and abridged by N.J.Dawood)

İbrahim Kalın
Ben, Öteki ve Ötesi
İdris Küçükömer
Düzenin Yabancılaşması, Cuntacılıktan Sivil Topluma
İlber Ortaylı
Türkiye Teşkilat ve İdare Tarihi - İmparatorluğun En Uzun Yılı - Türklerin Tarihi, 1923-2023 - Cumhuriyetin İlk Yüzyılı (İsmail Küçükkaya ile birlikte) - Osmanlıyı Yeniden Keşfetmek
İsmail Cem
Türkiye'de Geri Kalmışlığın Tarihi
İsmet Özel
Üç Mesele – Teknik, Medeniyet, Yabancılaşma
Jared Diamond
Guns, Germs and Steel - The Fates of Human Societies
Kadir Canatan
Şerif Mardin Eleştirisi
Kemal Karpat
Osmanlı'dan Günümüze Asker ve Siyaset - The Ottoman State and its Place in World History
Levent Köker
Modernleşme, Kemalizm ve Demokrasi
Lord Kinross
The Ottoman Centuries - Atatürk
Martha Cottam, Elena Mastors, Thomas Preston, Beth Dietz
Introduction to Political Psychology
Max Weber
The Protestant Ethic and the Spirit of Capitalism
Metin And
Dionisos ve Anadolu Köylüsü

Metin Aydoğan
Yönetim Gelenekleri ve Türkler
Miles Hewstone
Mark Rubin, HazelWillis - Intergroup Bias
Muammer Yılmaz
Osmanlı'da Darbeler ve İsyanlar
Mustafa Armağan
İlber Ortaylı İle Tarihin Derinlerine Yolculuk
Mustafa İnal
Askerî İsyanlar, Darbeler ve Ara Dönemlerin Perde Arkası
Mümtaz Turhan
Kültür Değişmeleri, Garblılaşmanın Neresindeyiz - Atatürk İlkeleri ve Kalkınma Sosyal Psikoloji Bakımından bir Tetkik
Nevzat Tarhan
Toplum Psikolojisi
Niall Ferguson
The West and the Rest
Niccolo Macchiavelli
Hükümdar
Nihal Atsız
Türk Edebiyatı Tarihi
Nilüfer Göle
Modern Mahrem - Toplumun Merkezine Yolculuk
Niyazi Berkes
Türkiye'de Çağdaşlaşma
Nur Vergin
Din, Toplum Ve Siyasal Sistem
Oktay Sinanoğlu
Bye Bye Türkçe
Olivier Roy

Siyasal İslam'ın İflası
Orhan Pamuk
Cevdet Bey ve Oğulları
Orhan Türkdoğan
Türk Toplum Sistemi ve Yapısal Sorunları
Özcan Köknel
İnsanı Anlamak - Kaygıdan Mutluluğa - Kişilik - Peyami Safa ve Falih Rıfkı Atay'da Halkın İnşası
Rene Grousset
The Empire of the Steppes of Central Asia
Reşad Ekrem Koçu
Yeniçeriler
Rıza Zelyut
Yabancı Kaynaklara Göre Türk Kimliği
Robin Lane Fox
Alexander the Great
Robert Kaplan
The Ends of the Earth - From Togo to Turkmenistan – From Iran to Cambodia - A Journey to the Frontiers of Anarchy
Sabri Ülgener
Zihniyet ve Din
Sabahattin Şen
Türk Aydını ve Kimlik Sorunu
Samuel P. Huntington
Clash of Civilizations
Sencer Divitçioğlu
Asya Üretim Tarzı ve Osmanlı Toplumu - Orta Asya Türk Tarihi Üzerine Altı Çalışma
Selim Hilmi Özkan
Osmanlı Tarihi I (1299-1774) Siyasi Tarih - Kültür ve Medeniyet, (Editör) - Osmanlı Toplum Yapısı

Sezai Karakoç
Diriliş Neslinin Âmentüsü
Sigmund Freud
Totem and Taboo - Uygarlığın Huzursuzluğu - Kitle Psikolojisi - Psikanaliz Üzerine
Stanford Shaw, Ezel Kural Shaw
Osmanlı İmparatorluğu ve Modern Türkiye
Stefanos Yerasimos
Az Gelişmişlik Sürecinde Türkiye
Suraiya Faroqhi
Osmanlı Kültürü ve Gündelik Yaşam, Ortaçağdan Yirminci Yüzyıla
Şerif Mardin
Türk Modernleşmesi - Makaleler IV - Din ve İdeoloji - Türkiye, İslâm ve Sekülarizm - Cuntacılıktan Sivil Topluma - Religion And Social Change In Modern Turkey
Şevket Pamuk
Türkiye'nin 200 Yıllık İktisadi Tarihi
Şeyda Büyükcan Sayılır
Türklerde Evren/Kâinat Anlayışı
Şevket Süreyya Aydemir
Tek Adam (Mustafa Kemal'in Hayatı) Üç cilt (biyografi) - İkinci Adam (İsmet Inonu) Üç cilt (biyografi) - Makedonya'dan Ortaasya'ya Enver Paşa Üç cilt (biyografi) - Suyu Arayan Adam (otobiyografi) - Menderes'in Dramı (biyografi) - İhtilalin Mantığı ve 27 Mayıs İhtilali (inceleme)
Şükrü Hanioğlu
Atatürk An Intellectual Biography
Taha Akyol

Ama Hangi Atatürk
Taner Timur
Osmanlı Kimliği, AKP'nin önlenebilir Karşı-Devrimi
Tezcan Durna
Kemalist Modernleşme ve Seçkincilik
Talat Tekin
Türk Dilleri Ailesi
Tuncay Önder
Türkiye'de Bürokrasi-Demokrasi İlişkisi Üzerine
Tuncer Baykara
Türk, Türklük ve Türkler
Umay Türkeş Günay
Türklerin Tarihi – Geçmişten Geleceğe
Vamık Volkan
Atatürk'ün Psikanalitik Biyografisi
V.V. Barthold
Orta Asya Türk Tarihi
Vedat Koçal
Çevre'den 'Merkez'e Yönelim Bağlamında, Türkiye'de Muhafazakârlığın, Dönüşümü: Siyasal İslâmcılıktan Muhafazakâr, Demokratlığa AK Parti Örneği
Yusuf Halaçoğlu
XIV-XVII. Yüzyıllarda Osmanlılarda Devlet Teşkilatı ve Sosyal Yapı
Yakup Kadri Karaosmanoğlu
Yaban
Zafer Toprak
Türkiye'de Yeni Hayat
Zülfü Livaneli
Serenad - Kaplanın Sırtında
Ziya Gokalp
Türkçülüğün Esasları

ABOUT THE AUTHOR

Ambassador Aydın Nurhan was born in Adapazarı in 1949.

He is a graduate of Talas American Secondary School, Tarsus American College and Ankara University Faculty of Law. Before entering the Ministry of Foreign Affairs, he worked as a lawyer registered with the Ankara Bar Association.

Starting with his last mission ending his career in 2017; upon the recommendation of the Ministry of Foreign Affairs of Türkiye, he was appointed as the Permanent Representative of the Organization of Islamic Cooperation to Afghanistan.

Earlier, he was the Ambassador of the Republic of Türkiye in Ghana, also accredited to Togo and Benin, Consul General in Azerbaijan, Austria and Australia. He was the Director General of Science and Technology at the Organization of Islamic Cooperation, and also served in Saudi Arabia, Holland, Germany and the United States in his junior years.

In his last posting at the headquarters, he was the acting Chairman of the Center for Strategic Studies of the Ministry of Foreign Affairs of Turkey. He was also among the diplomatic core serving in the establishing years of Turkish International Cooperation Agency TICA.

Apart from his diplomatic career, Mr. Nurhan was a TV commentator, media columnist, radio programmer and speaker, and university lecturer with an honorary doctorate.

Some of his lectures were published in the USA, Türkiye and Ghana. His article titled "Strategic Research Culture in Developing Countries" was published in the book "Strategic Thinking Culture and Strategic Research Centers in Turkey: Turkish Think Tanks from the Beginning to the Present".

His speeches and articles in Turkish and English are compiled in two books:

"Bir Büyükelçinin Düşünce Dünyası"
"Reflections of a Turkish Ambassador"

He was the recipient of the Medal of the National Order of the Republic of Benin, Honorary Doctorate of Nakhchevan Private University.

Aydın Nurhan is married and has two children.

www.ingramcontent.com/pod-product-compliance
Lightning Source LLC
Chambersburg PA
CBHW071306110526
44591CB00010B/803